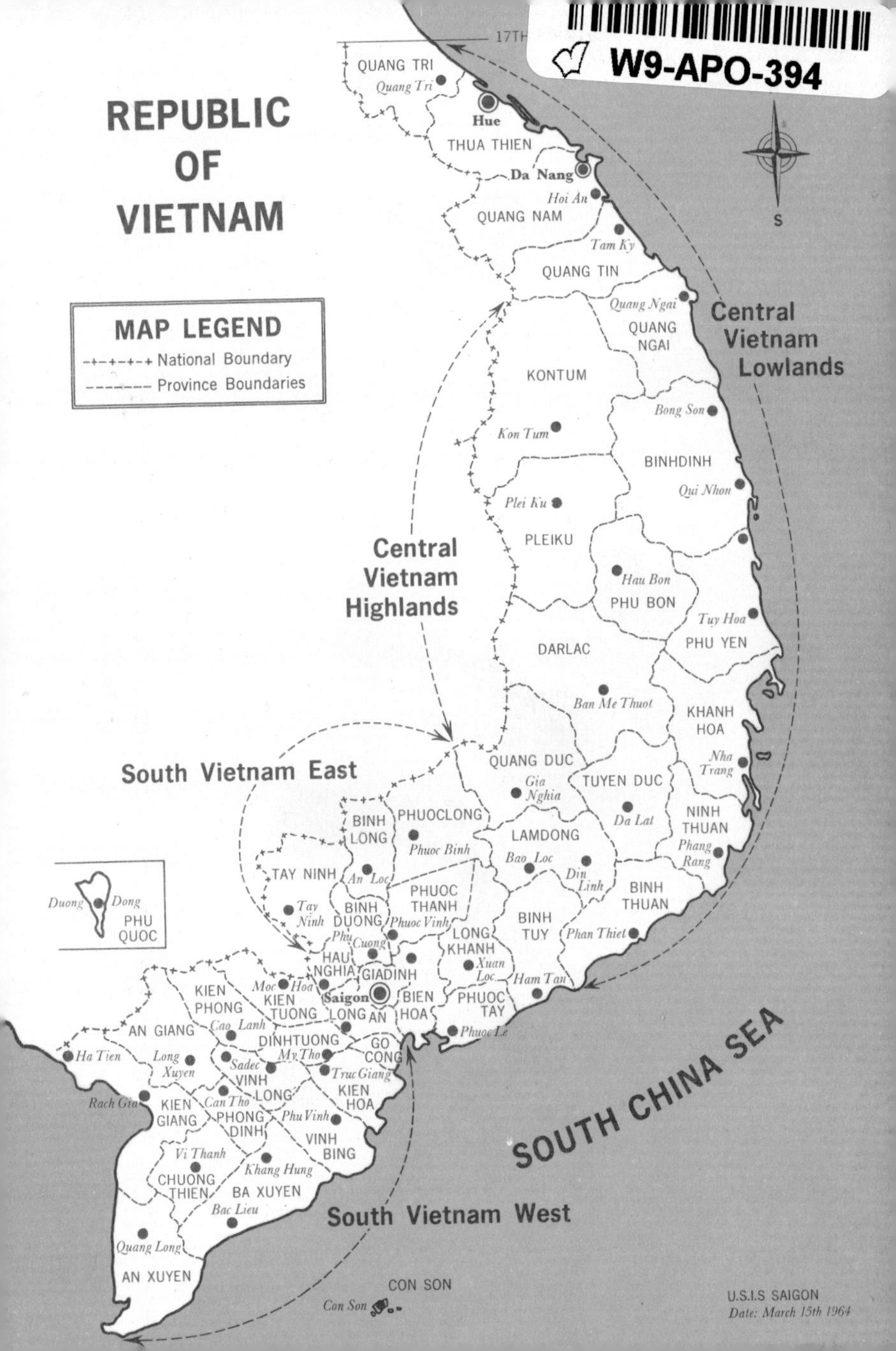
REPUBLIC OF VIETNAM
MAP LEGEND
National Boundary
Province Boundaries
17TH
QUANG TRI
Quang Tri
Hue
THUA THIEN
Da Nang
Hoi An
QUANG NAM
Tam Ky
QUANG TIN
Quang Ngai
QUANG NGAI
Central Vietnam Lowlands
KONTUM
Kon Tum
Bong Son
BINHDINH
Qui Nhon
Plei Ku
PLEIKU
Central Vietnam Highlands
Hau Bon
PHU BON
Tuy Hoa
PHU YEN
DARLAC
Ban Me Thuot
KHANH HOA
Nha Trang
QUANG DUC
Gia Nghia
TUYEN DUC
Da Lat
NINH THUAN
Phang Rang
South Vietnam East
BINH LONG
PHUOCLONG
Phuoc Binh
LAMDONG
Bao Loc
Din Linh
TAY NINH
An Loc
PHUOC THANH
Duong Dong
PHU QUOC
Tay Ninh
BINH DUONG
Phuoc Vinh
BINH TUY
BINH THUAN
Phu Cuong
LONG KHANH
Phan Thiet
HAU NGHIA
GIADINH
Xuan Loc
Ham Tan
KIEN PHONG
Moc Hoa
KIEN TUONG
Saigon
BIEN HOA
PHUOC TAY
AN GIANG
Cao Lanh
LONG AN
DINHTUONG
GO CONG
Phuoc Le
Ha Tien
Long Xuyen
Sadec
My Tho
Truc Giang
VINH LONG
KIEN HOA
Rach Gia
KIEN GIANG
Can Tho
PHONG DINH
Phu Vinh
VINH BING
Vi Thanh
Khang Hung
CHUONG THIEN
BA XUYEN
Bac Lieu
SOUTH CHINA SEA
South Vietnam West
Quang Long
AN XUYEN
CON SON
Con Son
U.S.I.S SAIGON
Date: March 15th 1964

Customs and Culture of
VIETNAM

Customs and Culture of

VIETNAM

by Ann Caddell Crawford

Illustrations by Hau Dinh Cam

CHARLES E. TUTTLE CO.: PUBLISHERS
Rutland, Vermont & Tokyo, Japan

Representatives
Continental Europe: BOXERBOOKS, INC., *Zurich*
British Isles: PRENTICE-HALL INTERNATIONAL, INC., *London*
Australasia: PAUL FLESCH & CO., PTY. LTD., *Melbourne*
Canada: M. G. HURTIG LTD., *Edmonton*

Published by the Charles E. Tuttle Co., Inc.
of Rutland, Vermont & Tokyo, Japan
with editorial offices at
Suido 1-chome, 2-6, Bunkyo-ku, Tokyo

Library of Congress
Catalog Card No. 66-16721

First edition, 1966
Eighth printing, 1968

Book design & typography by Keiko Chiba

PRINTED IN JAPAN

DEDICATION

To my husband
Major William R. Crawford
and my mother
Mrs. Carl Lamar Caddell Sr.

CONTENTS

FOREWORD

ANN CRAWFORD's book on the customs and culture of Vietnam fulfills a need for a source book of basic information on a nation which was unknown to Americans a few years ago but which is now the object of national attention.

To Americans who come to Vietnam without having first aquainted themselves with the customs of this ancient nation, Mrs. Crawford's highly readable book will be of great assistance.

To some persons, an assignment to a foreign land where the people and the customs appear to be extremely different impels exclusive association with other Americans, reliance on American food and isolation of oneself from one's surroundings.

Such an attitude is a mistake, not only for the sake of the individual himself but also for the sake of his work.

Customs and Culture of Vietnam is a book which will prevent an American from having the feeling that there is an unbridgeable gap between himself and his Southeast Asian surroundings. Even in the midst of war those of us who have the privilege of working and living with the Vietnamese can find an opportunity to learn about the many rich and interesting traditions of this country as well as to admire the courage of people who have survived in spite of so many attempts to conquer them.

Ann Crawford's excellent guide is a good place for an American to start his Vietnamese education.

HENRY CABOT LODGE

PREFACE AND ACKNOWLEDGMENTS

HARDLY a day goes by that we do not hear of the war in Vietnam and the debate that it has brought forth throughout the world. The things we hear little about, however, are the people, their heritage, and their daily life.

Before I went to Vietnam, I searched the public libraries for information and found very little available. This book is a result of that frustration. I hope that it will be of use to others, especially to students who are asked to write term papers on the country.

After studying Vietnam and its people first-hand for two years, I have attempted to choose a sampling of things which I hope will help the reader to understand the people of that country better. It is impossible to include everything of importance that I gathered in my research in a book of this nature; therefore, for the avid student of Vietnam, a selected list of references are included in the Appendices.

Limited information is included on North Vietnam today and many statistics quoted are for South Vietnam only. The majority of the information about customs and culture applies to all Vietnamese living on both sides of the 17th parallel. The government of North Vietnam did not reply to my queries on the country, and little printed documentation can be found about it in the free world.

Numerous people have helped me obtain information for this book. First of all, I would like to thank all of those people in Vietnam who were so anxious to see that their country be known to others in lands far away. They include my students in Vietnam, the Vietnamese librarians, Vietnamese personnel working for the United States Information Service, employees of the Vietnamese Ministry of Information, especially Mr. Doan Bich, and our foster daughter, Miss Hau Dinh Cam, who worked very hard typing borrowed copies of single documents, before and after translations, and for illustrating this book.

Next, my thanks is extended to Americans who encouraged me in my efforts and who made comprehensive statistics available to me from official U.S. agencies in Vietnam. Whenever I travelled outside of Saigon, there were numerous Americans in the armed services and other officials agencies who went out of their way to introduce me to Vietnamese who were knowledgeable about the area and its customs.

Appreciation is also extended to Major Grace Johancen, Public Information Officer, Fort Lee, Virginia, for her valuable proof-reading and editorial assistance which was freely given in her off-duty hours.

A special thanks goes to the numerous missionaries stationed in Vietnam, who have perhaps the best understanding of the people and their customs of any foreigners living there.

Last, but not least, I would like to thank my husband and my children for their interest and proddings, without which I might have given up on numerous perplexing occasions. For my children, I am grateful for their innate curiosity and their facility for getting me into numerous conversations with the Vietnamese. To my husband, Roy, goes a special thanks for never holding me back even when some of the things I did in Vietnam might have seemed to be a little crazy or even dangerous. I am thankful for his unselfishness and understanding.

I am also grateful to the United States Army which sent my husband to Vietnam and later allowed the children and me to join him. What at first seemed to be a disappointment (we had orders to go to Arizona which were cancelled) turned out to be one of the most interesting and challenging experiences in our life and one that we will never forget.

ANN CADDELL CRAWFORD

Fort Lee, Virginia

CHAPTER 1

WILL THE TWAIN MEET?

"East is East and West is West
and never the twain shall meet."
Rudyard Kipling

NEARLY all of the first Western ventures in Vietnam ended in failure or disappointment. For the most part, the reasons for these misfortunes could well be attributed to the desire of one foreign power to enforce its domination on the country, or a lack of understanding in the case of individual events.

Today, the West is no longer interested in colonization. The French and their power in Vietnam has almost disappeared.

The Vietnamese, a fiercely independent race, have thrown out one foreign power after another; including Chinese, Mongols, and French. In addition, they pushed the Cambodians and the Chams out of territory that they occupied.

These events have been accomplished despite the fact that the Vietnamese were outnumbered on many occasions.

The North Vietnamese communists prey on this past history in their propaganda today, and try to identify the Americans and other foreigners working in South Vietnam with the former ruling powers. They tell the Vietnamese that these foreigners must be driven out, just as the French and the Chinese were expelled—by force.

Time will tell if the Western powers can prove to these people, as well as others watching in underdeveloped nations around the world, that they are not interested in anything in the country except keeping it from falling under communist domination. This problem, though sticky, may be far easier to reckon with than the other problem; that of a lack of understanding, which like a cancer, slowly eats away at the heart of a nation until all vital points are rendered useless.

Lack of understanding can occur in numerous ways. The first problem results from a powerful government action; the second may result from individuals of various stations in life, from the lowest private in the armed forces to the highest ranking government officers.

It may be caused unintentionally such as in a theme written by one of my Vietnamese students. He wrote of an American who had visited a local Buddhist pagoda. While there, he became surrounded by little children, all holding out their hands asking for money or candy. The American GI wanted to give them something, but how do you give something to a hundred kids? He returned to his Special Services chartered bus and waved goodbye to the children. They all pressed around the window shouting the few words of English they knew. Smiling, the GI reached into his pocket and pulled out a whole handful of Vietnamese coins and as the bus pulled off threw them out the window to the children. This resulted in a stampede with the children fighting each other for the coins. The older Vietnamese standing by looked on in disgust as if to say, "Who do those Americans think they are, making beggars of our children?"

The First American in Vietnam

The first American to venture to Vietnam was John White of Marblehead, Massachusetts. He failed to reach an understanding with the Vietnamese and returned home disgusted. White arrived in Vietnam in 1819 on a ship named THE FRANKLIN. He was delayed in accomplishing his business of setting up trade between the Vietnamese and the Americans, by the countless idiosyncrasies of the Vietnamese. White was repulsed by the people's habits which he considered barbarian. Had he known what to expect, he might have been better prepared to understand and deal with them.

He performed a valuable service to other Americans following him, however, by recording his impressions of the people and the country in a book entitled, *History of a Voyage to the China Sea.* This book may be found in the Library of Congress in the United States, at Washington, D.C.

The First American Diplomat in Vietnam

Edmund Roberts, a navigator from New England with far east travel experience, was selected by President Andrew Jackson in March, 1832, for the first official mission to Vietnam.

Despite a few technical errors in paperwork, the visit went

well and the Emperor Minh Mang wrote, "If their country wishes to establish commercial relations, we do not see any objections to it provided they respect our laws." This paved the way for more formal negotiations four year's later.

When Roberts returned on the next visit, all did not go well. Upon the American's request for an audience, the emperor said to Vice-President of the Ministry of Finance, Dao-Tri-Phu, "Considering their courteous and peaceable attitude, would it not be advisable to accede to their request?"

Dao-Tri-Phu suggested that they should entertain the visitors for awhile and try to learn their real intentions.

There was a dissenter, however. The Vice-President of the cabinet, Hoang-Quynh, warned, "Their country is cunning and crafty, and we should not comply with their requests. If we commit ourselves without due consideration, we shall have much trouble in the future. Our ancestors used to close off the frontiers and refuse contact with the West; it was a good policy."

Nevertheless, the emperor declared, "They have come from many leagues beyond the seas, thus proving their admiration for our virtue and the prestige of our court. How can we reject them? If we do, we would display a lack of magnanimity."

Unfortunately for both sides, when the high ranking mission went to see the Americans on board ship, they were told that there was illness on board and they could not be received. Later, the Americans suddenly left without advising the court. Dao-Tri-Phu, the Vice-President of the Ministry of Finance, reported back to the emperor stating, "These fugitives have proved how uncivil they are."

The Emperor Minh Mang, wrote in his report, "They came to us without our rejecting them; they left without our sending them; we have conducted ourselves in accordance with Chinese courtesy. We do not need to take offense when we are dealing with foreign barbarians."

It is unfortunate that the Vietnamese were not acquainted with the reason for the sudden departure of the Americans. Roberts had been taken acutely ill and was deteriorating rapidly. His assistant, a US Navy surgeon, made a hasty departure to find additional medical help for Roberts. It was in vain as Roberts died in Macao on June 12, 1836.

Despite the fact that both the Vietnamese and the Americans had good intentions, a misunderstanding caused the second mission from the United States to Vietnam to end in a sad manner for both countries.

The First Vietnamese Envoy to the United States

In 1837, Vietnam was disputing the right of France to control all of Vietnam. The Vietnamese emperor hoped to get help from the United States and sent their country's first envoy to the United States. He chose Bui-Vien for the important post. Bui-Vien was a scholar and well respected in Vietnam. Before his departure, he was personally received by the Emperor Tu Duc, who impressed upon him the grave importance of his mission.

After a lot of red tape, Bui-Vien was received in the United States by President Ulysses S. Grant. The President assured the Vietnamese envoy of American interest and assistance, but stated that he must have credentials which would enable him to justify any action he might present to the American

Congress. Bui-Vien left for Vietnam to get the emperor to provide him with the important diplomatic documents.

On his way home, he received news that President Grant could not honor his offer to help, because of new political circumstances. Bui-Vien was bitterly disappointed to see his hopes of American aid for Vietnam fade away.

On reaching Japan, Bui-Vien met with a friend of his, the American consul. They exchanged poems with each other, one of which is indicative of Bui-Vien's feelings. He said in part:

> *"We pour our wine into glasses at Yokohama in the ninth month of autumn.*
> *Turning my head towards the clouds of Vietnam*
> *I feel extremely anxious about my country.*
> *Sea and land, memory and emotion remind me of my former journeys.*
> *Enjoying myself with you, I regret all the more that we must part,*
> *Spiritual companion! In what year will we be together in the same sampan?"*

In the Same Sampan

Today, Bui-Vien's question has at last received an answer. The United States and a few other countries of the Western world, are now in the same sampan with South Vietnam. The new question for modern-day poets may well be, "Can understanding be achieved, and can the sampan be kept afloat?"

The answer, in my opinion, now depends on the ordinary Vietnamese villager, not the big politicians or even the leader of the country. It also depends on understanding between the Americans and their allies and the Vietnamese.

Americans working at the "ground level" with Vietnamese have an important impact on understanding. In the eyes of the Vietnamese villager, each American represents the United States.

Another saying goes, "There is a great wall between the Orient and the Occident; it is not the wall of China, but rather the wall of misunderstanding." Seldom, if ever, do two diverse cultures meet on a common ground. The road to understanding is a two-way street. Here's hoping that this book will help bridge that gap of lack of understanding on our side of the road. We can only go so far, however. The Vietnamese must meet us somewhere along the way.

CHAPTER

2

THE COUNTRY

Geography Vietnam lies between 8°33′ and 23°22′ north latitude. It is bordered on the north by China; on the south by the Gulf of Siam; on the east by the Gulf of Tonkin and the South China Sea for more than 1400 miles; and on the west by Cambodia and Laos.

The Republic of Vietnam (South Vietnam) and the Democratic Republic of Vietnam (North Vietnam) are divided at approximately the 17th parallel by a narrow demilitarized zone along the Song Ben Hai river. At this point of division, the country is only 39 miles wide.

This distance gradually widens in the south until it reaches approximately 100 miles across at the Laos, Cambodia, and Vietnam border. The widest point in the south is along an east-west line between the port town of Phan Rang on the South China Sea and near Hoa Hiep on the Cambodian border where the distance is 210 miles.

The widest point in the north is approximately 350 miles from the Laos border to the Gulf of Tonkin at the base of South China.

The shape of North and South Vietnam together is like a big "S." South Vietnam is similar to the reverse shape of California and is smaller than that state.

Total land area of the whole country, north and south, is approximately 127,000 square miles. South Vietnam is about 65,000 square miles, a little smaller than the state of Washington. North Vietnam makes up the remaining 62,000 square miles.

Description Vietnam is a land of diversity. In this beautiful country, one may find mountains; plains alternating with deep valleys; cultivated green fields; and sparsely settled savanna lands. Even small areas of land resembling deserts are found in Vietnam. About half of the country is jungle, with 80 per cent of the land covered with trees and bushes.

Central Vietnam is characterized by a chain of mountains, ranging in height from 3,500 to 10,000 feet.

One of the most common Vietnamese descriptions of their country, is that it looks like a bamboo pole holding a bucket of rice on each end.

Lush rice lands are found both in the delta of South Vietnam along the Mekong river, and in North Vietnam along the delta of the Red River. Consequently, this is why it is described as a bamboo pole with two big rice bowls on each end of the country. The pole is the long, slender part of Vietnam characterized by the mountain ranges.

Central Vietnam does not enjoy the fertile lands that are

found in the north and south. It is like a long irregular corridor joining the north and south. Made up of small hill plains and mountains, it is drained by relatively short streams.

There are many picturesque scenes and enjoyable cities in Central Vietnam including the most important city of the south, Saigon.

In sharp contrast with the deltas displaying seasonal crops are the tropical forests, providing a natural habitat for countless wild animals.

In the central area of the country, which is not suitable for agriculture, rubber plantations abound in the rich volcanic soil.

Population The population range for South Vietnam is 15 to 16 million people. In the north, it is 16 to 17 million.

The majority of people in Vietnam live in the rice-producing regions. The Red River delta in North Vietnam is more heavily populated than the delta region of the Mekong in the south. As many as 1,000 to 3,000 people may live on one square mile of land in the Red River delta. Figures for the southern delta show between 200 to 500 people residing on one square mile of land. In the mountain regions of Vietnam, as few as five or six people may live on a square mile of land.

Hydrography The principal river of North Vietnam is the Red River (Son Hong Ha) which begins in the Yunnan province of China and flows through North Vietnam spreading into a delta before emptying into the Gulf of Tonkin. It is sometimes called the "mother river" because its alluvium fertilizes the lands of North Vietnam. Other rivers are the Clear River (Lo-Giang) and the Black River (Da-Giang). Main streams are the Day, the River of Nam-Dinh, the Canal of Rapids and the Canal of Bamboos.

The Red River delta is joined to another, the Song Tai-Binh which is made up of the three united rivers, the Cau, Thuong, and Luc-Nam.

The best-known river in the central region is the Perfume River in Hue province. Other small rivers abound in this area including the Ca, Ma, Gianh, Thu Bon, Tra-Khuc, and Da-Rang.

By far the most important river in the southern part of the country is the huge Mekong, which winds over 2,500 miles from the highlands in Tibet to the South China Sea. The entire delta region of South Vietnam is furrowed by many streams, tributaries of larger rivers and numerous canals which make up an excellent network for navigation and irrigation.

Some of the other rivers and streams in the south are the Dong Na (splits into the Donnai and River of Saigon); the Vam-Co and the branches of the Mekong, Tien-Giang (upper river) and the Hau-Giang (lower river).

Climate

The climate of Vietnam, just as its geography, is subject to many variations.

North Vietnam

The climate in the north is very similar to that of southern China. It is characterized by great seasonal differences in temperature, and sudden changes are not uncommon.

There are two main seasons in North Vietnam, winter and summer. Winter generally lasts from November to April with rather pleasant cool weather. The average temperature in this season is about 60°F. This season is usually rather dry. The summer season begins in May and lasts till October. It is a time of tremendous heat, heavy rainfall, and typhoons. The average temperatures range between 86° and 89°F. The daily temperatures may run in the 90's during this season.

South Vietnam

The south has a monsoon climate with rather consistent average temperatures of between 77° and 86°. There are two main seasons—wet and dry. The dry season lasts from November to April with barely a day of rain and then changes to the rainy season which lasts from May to October.

November is usually the month of transition. There is an exception to this in the region of Phan Thiet to Phan Rang where the rains come from September to December. Typhoons are common along the coast between July and November.

The hottest and most unpleasant time in South Vietnam is generally between February and April when the atmosphere is humid and the many storms seldom break into a cooling rain.

In Central Vietnam, the climate is a transition between the climates of the north and south.

HOTTEST MONTHS

North Vietnam	June, July, and August.
South Vietnam	March, April, and May.

AVERAGE ANNUAL TEMPERATURES

SAIGON Between 77° and 86°.
The lowest temperature ever recorded in Saigon was 57°. Mean maximum temperature is approximately 95° in April. Mean minimum—approximately 70° in January.

DALAT Temperatures here are considerably lower with a 60°–70° range in winter. The highs and lows for the year are around 80° and 40°. Ideal weather is from November to March, during the dry season.

HUE Between 68° and 86°.

HANOI Between 63° and 86°.

Rainfall Rainfall in Vietnam is heavy. The yearly average is about 59 inches. The maximum annual amount of rain is usually registered at Hue where it often reaches 110 inches. At Hanoi, the rains begin at the end of May and reach their height in August, with 14 inches for that month. The dryest region is Cap Padaran where the yearly amount is only three inches.

Saigon's monthly rainfall average during the rainy season is approximately 50 inches.

WILDLIFE

Flora As in all tropical countries, Vietnam has a range of plants that vary from those of great beauty to those of danger. It has been reported that more than 2,000 varieties of orchid grow wild in the jungles of Vietnam. Beautiful flowers can be found in gardens year-round in the cooler areas of the country such as Dalat and other mountain areas.

The Botanical Gardens in Saigon has one of the best collections of orchids and equatorial plants in the world.

There are also dangerous plants such as several species of poisonous nettles growing in the southern part of the country. They grow to a height of 10 to 15 feet and have pointed, heart-shaped leaves with serrated edges which contain poisonous hairs. Contact with these plants causes a painful skin eruption.

Another item of special interest is the sack tree *(Antiarus Toxicaria)* which has a poisonous sap. Natives and Viet-Cong use the sap for arrow poison. The tree grows to a height of 100 feet and its leaves are similar to those of an elm.

Fauna There are up to 500 species of fauna in Vietnam. Except for urban and built-up areas, the country is one big hunting ground. Indeed, in times of peace, it could be the hunting paradise of Asia.

The favorites of big-game hunters include tigers, panthers, elephants, wild oxen and buffalo, boars, bears, deer, *capicorns,* Cambodian *roe, koupreys,* and others. Small game include birds ranging from the peacock to the partridge.

A popular small animal caught by the use of a snare is the mouse-deer.

There are also many monkeys in the Vietnamese forests, and each year thousands are exported for medical research.

Two of the most outstanding zoo's in the country are located in Saigon and Dalat. The zoo at Dalat is small but impressive. It is located inside a forest reserve and the animals can be observed in their natural habitat.

Snakes There are more than 60 known species of snakes, 20 of them poisonous. They include cobras, kraits, vipers, and water snakes.

Caimans Pythons and caimans are hunted for their skins which have great value. Alligators are often a threat to villagers, especially in the south.

Turtles There are various species of turtles in the country, but the caret, common around islands, is popular because its shell can be used for handicrafts.

Rodents Rodents are a problem for farmers and housewives. There are great numbers of rats, mice, moles, squirrels, etc., and some rats are as big as house cats.

Fish In addition to the species described in Chapter 9, there are several kinds of fish that can inject venom through their spines, causing painful stings and sometimes death. Sharks are also prevalent along the coast.

Leeches One of the worst pests of the jungle is the land leech which inhabits the grass and underbrush. Its bite is not venomous or painful, but causes bleeding, and infection can develop ulcers at the wound. They are usually removed by burning, as one removes a tick from a dog.

Mollusks Snails are found in great abundance, especially along the paddy fields and waterways. Serious diseases can be contacted from them as they act as a carrier of blood parasites. In the southern coastal waters, there are also a few species of marine mollusks which can inflict painful and sometimes fatal stings.

Mosquitoes Numerous species of mosquitoes reside in Vietnam, many of which transmit diseases such as malaria, dengue fever, and hemmorraghic fever. A tremendous program aimed at eliminating malaria was working well until the Vietnamese personnel carrying out the spraying became the object of Viet-Cong terrorism.

Insects Many people are infested with lice and it is a common sight to see the Vietnamese picking them from each other's hair. Fleas, ticks, mites, spiders, scorpions, ants, termites, bedbugs, and cockroaches are all present in the country.

HISTORY IN A NUTSHELL

THE EARLIEST history of Vietnam is shrouded in legend, all of which has been violent and politically turbulent.

According to one account, Vietnam was begun when a dragon mated with a goddess who "laid one hundred eggs" from which were born an equal number of sons.

By another version, Chen Nong, one of the founders of the Chinese civilization, had a grandson named King De Minh. This grandson made an inspection tour in the "South" and while there married a "mortal." Their eldest children were given the northern empire (or China) and the youngest,

King Duong Vuong, was made "King of the South" and formed the first Vietnamese dynasty. The land is believed to have been absorbed in what is China today.

One of King Duong Vuong's sons, Lac Long Quan, was supposed to have married the daughter of a neighboring prince, and she "laid a hundred eggs" from which were born the same number of sons.

According to legend, Lac Long Quan gave 50 sons to their mother and kept 50 for himself. The eldest of these 50 sons came to the throne as the first in a line of 18 princes. All of them had the same name or title, Hung Vuong, and were distinguished by numbers.

Because of this legendary beginning, many Vietnamese consider themselves related to each other.

The oldest inhabitants of what is Vietnam today were most likely the Chams, a few thousand of whom still remain among the mountain people.

These mountain tribes reflect migrations from all directions having some relationship in language and handicrafts to Lao, Cambodian, Thai, Chinese, Malay, Indonesian, Philippine, and other Pacific island races. The southern areas of Vietnam reflect migrations from China. The Chams, who had a rather high development of culture, were later completely defeated by the Vietnamese after years of warfare which was originally initiated by the Chinese governors of Vietnam.

Vietnam has been ruled off and on by China throughout the centuries and this partly accounts for their resistance to China today.

Beginning before the birth of Christ, the Chinese began

a series of invasions intent on controlling the rich rice-producing lands of the south. Among the first people in Vietnam that they conquered were the "Giao-Chi," a group of scattered nomadic tribes which had migrated from eastern Tibet. Because of these invasions by the Chinese and the resulting occupations and migrations, culture in Vietnam has been greatly influenced by the Chinese.

Despite this influence, the Vietnamese people have shown a desire to hang on to what is theirs and theirs alone. Their language and determination to remain a separate entity and wholly Vietnamese has survived.

The last attempt by the Chinese to invade Vietnam was in 1788. By this time, Portuguese and French missionaries and European explorers had begun to leave an imprint of Western civilization upon the people of Vietnam. The Portuguese traders who set up a trading station near Da-Nang (Tourane) in the 16th century, were the earliest known Western contacts with the Vietnamese. They were swiftly followed by the Spanish, Dutch, English, and French, all of whom have left a little of their culture behind. Their ventures in the country, however, may take up only a page in the history of Vietnam.

For simplification, a Vietnamese historian has divided the history of Vietnam into five era's.

First establishment of the nation: 2,879 B.C. to 111 B.C.
Chinese domination: 111 B.C. to A.D. 938
The great national dynasties: 939–1883
French Administration: 1883–1954
Post-World War II Period: After 1945

The Early Settlement of the Vietnamese Nation

Historians state that the Vietnamese nation was established in the first millennium B.C., mainly by the Viets who emigrated from Central China. This is a period rich in legend, the telling of which gets better and more exciting with each succeeding generation. The area became known as the Kingdom of Nam Viet in 207 B.C.

Chinese Domination

Vietnam fell under the domination of its neighbor China in 111 B.C. when Lo Bac Duc, a Chinese general, destroyed Nam Viet. This period of domination continued until A.D. 938 with the exception of two short-lived revolutions.

The first rebellion was led by the famous Trung sisters, Trung Trac and Trung Nhi, idolized to this day in Vietnam. Leading their armies in a successful revolt, they restored the country's independence for three years. They were later defeated by large Chinese forces. The sisters then committed suicide by drowning themselves in a river. More information about them may be found in Chapter 10.

The second successful rebellion was led by Ly Nam De. He reigned over the liberated country from A.D. 544–602.

During the Chinese period of domination in Vietnam, much of the Chinese culture was absorbed by the Vietnamese nation.

Two famous Chinese governors of this era were Tich Quang and Nham-Diem.

The Chinese held their position in Vietnam later, despite the early dynasties of the Ly's, Trieu's, and others.

The Great National Dynasties

This particular era of independence for Vietnam lasted almost 1,000 years. The actual turning point from Chinese domition was established when Ngo-Quyen defeated the Chinese armies on the Bach-Dang River in 938. He became emperor of free Vietnam the next year and reigned until 967. Ngo-Quyen was succeeded by eight diferent royal dynasties:

Dinh Dynasty	967–968
Le Dynasty	980–1009
Ly Dynasty	1010–1224
Tran Dynasty	1225–1400
Ho Dynasty	1400–1407
Posterior Le Dynasty	1428–1788
Tay Son Dynasty	1788–1802
Nguyen Dynasty	1802–1945

The Emperor Bao Dai was the last reigning descendant of the Nguyen Dynasty.

There are many things of historical importance which occurred during these dynasties.

Since the 11th century, under the Ly Dynasty, great progress was made. The country was unified; the economic, administrative and military organizations were greatly improved; cultural development commenced; and Buddhism was extended into Vietnam.

The famous Temple of Literature was built in Hanoi in 1070. The National University was created in 1076.

During these dynasties, Vietnamese armies turned back numerous invaders including the Chinese and the Mongols.

Due to internal strife, the Chinese were able to return and dominate Vietnam once more from 1407 to 1427.

One of Vietnam's national heroes, Le-Loi defeated the Chinese after a ten-year struggle. He ascended the throne under the reigning title of Le-Thai-To and gave the country the name of Dai-Viet and set up the capital at Hanoi, then called Dong-Do or Dong-Kinh.

There were also two partitions of Vietnam during these dynasties, similar to the one which exists today.

The first was from 1532 to 1592 when the Le Dynasty, which controlled the southern part of the country below Thanh-Hoa near the 20th parallel, fought the Mac Dynasty which occupied the north. The partition was ended by a victory for Le.

The second partition lasted from 1674 until 1802 when Gia-Long of the Nguyen family became emperor of a unified Vietnam once more.

The Era of the French Administration 1883-1954

Vietnam came in contact with the West, especially France, during the 19th century expansion of the West to Asia. Under the Nguyen Dynasties, hostilities broke out between France and Vietnam during the second half of the 19th century. The Vietnamese were overwhelmed by the French and were forced to yield their southern provinces in 1862 and 1867 as French colonies. This area was known as Cochin-China. The areas known as Annam and Tonkin were placed under the status of a French Protectorate in 1834.

Resistance, both active and passive, continued for a long time, however, and the French had to suppress many revolts.

Some of the most important were those led by Emperor Ham-Nghi (1885–88); nationalist leaders Phan Ding Phung (1893–95) and Hoang Hoa Tham (1889–1913); and the Nationalist Party in 1930.

The matter of France and Vietnam has long been a subject of debate. There are those who claim the French contributed a great deal to Vietnam, both with money and talent. Then there are also those who believe that Vietnam was exploited by France only as a provider of raw materials, yet was not given any opportunity for industrial development. The late President of the United States, Franklin D. Roosevelt believed this and was often quoted as saying that France had milked Vietnam dry, long enough.

The French ran the administration of Vietnam, and a Vietnamese historian charged that there was not a single Vietnamese as head of a province, a city, a battalion, or even as police commissioner when World War II broke out. He believed that this particularly made Vietnam an easy prey to communists and their subversion at the end of that war.

In Vietnam today, one can easily see the result of the French venture there. The second language is French and even the streets of the larger cities are built similar to those in France. This often leads to the comment that Saigon is the "Paris of the Orient." Architecture, medicine, administration and other things have continued to run as they did when the French were in power. Many Vietnamese citizens have been trained in France, and the Pasteur Institute stands today as a monument to the study of Asian diseases in Vietnam.

Chapter 5 contains more comprehensive information on the French influence in Vietnam, especially in the fields of civil service and education.

The Post-War II Period

The French continued to administer the country under Japanese military occupation which began in September 1940. For several years thereafter the French in Vietnam behaved with hospitality and cooperation toward the Japanese, thus protecting their investment in the country. At this same time, however, Americans were fighting to help save Free France in Europe and fighting the Japanese in the Pacific.

Toward the end of World War II, the Japanese made an "about face" and forcefully removed the French from the administration of Vietnam. Many French people lost their lives to the Japanese in Vietnam at this time. This left the country in a state of turmoil and without most public services, as these had been run by the French for over sixty years.

Some of the hard-feeling by the French for the United States today may be traced to the fact that the United States did not intercede immediately in the French people's behalf when the Japanese finally took action against them. On the other hand, many Americans did not understand the French cooperation and hospitable attitude toward the Japanese up to this point in Vietnam.

On April 16, 1945, a government was formed by Tran Trong Kim in an effort to restore law and order and to reorganize the country under Vietnamese administration. Even though the government was formed while still under Japanese occupation and during a world war, the new government formally declared that it was independent and "newborn" and that it wanted to be left alone for its reorganization.

According to Vietnamese historians, the Japanese refused to turn over the arms, money, tools, buildings, etc., that they had seized from the French. Without these things, the new government was helpless. Tran Trong Kim resigned about a week before the end of World War II. Emperor Bao-Dai abdicated on August 25, 1945, and a vacuum was created in the government, paving the way for further conflicts. In addition, the desire for national independence was a natural subterfuge for the communists in their attempts to take over the rice bowl of Asia.

The Viet-Minh "Viet-Minh" is an abbreviation for "Vietnam Doc Lap Dong Minh" or "League for the Independence of Vietnam." The organization was founded during World War II by Vietnamese refugees in China.

Evidently this was used as a front organization for the communists, for Nguyen Ai Quoc, one of its leaders, changed his name to Ho Chi Minh in order to conceal his communist past, as he knew that the Vietnamese had little interest in communism but wanted national independence.

Supposedly, the Viet-Minh were to act as underground agents against the Japanese during that time, and some Americans from our various secret agencies were even posted with them. In actuality, the Viet-Minh did not make outstanding progress in harming the Japanese.

Many Vietnamese nationalists were induced to join the Viet-Minh as they believed they were going to seek the independence of Vietnam.

Ho Chi Minh proclaimed his government in Hanoi on September 2, 1945, without having to fire a single shot.

When the French re-entered Vietnam, they found themselves at war with a group that had been armed in part by the Allies. Many of the Vietnamese chose to join their own government, even if it was a communist one, in order to drive the foreign power, France, out of their country for good.

The French installed the Emperor Bao Dai on March 8, 1949, promising independence within the French union. The whole set-up was rife with confusion, and graft was rampant. Instead of drawing the people to the French-run government, the opposite happened and more people joined the side of Ho Chi Minh.

Errors, lost battles, and a strange new kind of war led to the French forces defeat at Dien Bien Phu on May 8, 1954. The Vietnamese people fought to victory in spite of the superior French forces and fire power. They won, but unfortunately many of them were deceived. Those Vietnamese chose what they thought to be the lesser of two evils only to be trapped within communist subversion.

The end of French rule in Vietnam occurred when the Geneva Accords were signed in 1954 bringing colonial wars in the area to an end, and signalling the beginning of an even more dangerous, outright communist war.

The Geneva Accords Under the terms of the Geneva agreement, the northern part of Vietnam and about half of Central Vietnam came under communist control. The remainder of Central Vietnam and all the South became "free" and the Emperor Bao-Dai was its head of government at the time. Laos and Cambodia also became independent national states under the Geneva Accords.

One particular clause in the Accords provided that people in either zone could move to the other if they so desired. Approximately one million refugees flowed to the southern areas of Vietnam because they did not wish to live under communism. A good accounting of this mass movement is included in Dr. Thomas Dooley's book, *Deliver Us From Evil*. A few thousand southerners also moved north.

Viet-Cong Many communists remained in the south to raise their heads later when the Viet-Minh showed up once again, this time known as the Viet-Cong. (Viet communists represented by the National Liberation Front.)

Emperor Bao-Dai was deposed in 1955 and President Ngo Dinh Diem was installed by popular vote in the south.

The communists have continued in their efforts to weaken and destroy the government in South Vietnam and have wholeheartedly carried out their plans to conquer the south. In 1961, U.S. military aid was greatly increased to meet the challenge of the serious threat to the survival of the South Vietnamese people.

Viet-Cong terror tactics are known throughout the world today and many free nations led by the United States have joined hands with the South Vietnamese people to defeat the communists in South Vietnam. It is a difficult battle, but one that has received the determination to win from the United States under the leadership of Presidents Eisenhower, Kennedy, and Johnson.

Later Governments in South Vietnam President Diem's government started out well in South Vietnam and he became known in some circles as the "George Washington" of that country. He continued with a series of improvements for the citizens of Vietnam that would do credit to any leader. Unfortunately, he became more and more dictatorial, refused guidance from noted counselors and relied more and more on his brother Nhu, and his wife, Madame Nhu.

Gradually, the situation became worse. Two attempted coup d'etat's were foiled, but the third succeeded on November 1, 1963. Diem and his brother Nhu were captured, and both were killed by a dissident Major in the Army of Vietnam.

Diem was toppled by military means by a military junta led by an affable General Duong Van Minh. He, too, was replaced in a bloodless coup on January 30, 1964, by General Nguyen Khanh. General Khanh was also replaced after a see-sawing effort to stay in power.

Since that time there have been a number of civilian and military caretaker governments, only one of which has remained in power for an appreciable length of time. It is headed by South Vietnamese Premier Cao Ky, a flamboyant young officer who worked his way from Colonel to Vice Air Marshal and Premier of the country in a period of less than three years.

INTERESTING PEOPLE IN VIETNAM'S PAST

A NEW SAIGON resident can learn the names of Vietnam's heroes in a matter of weeks. Practically every street in the city is named for a famous person from Vietnam's colorful history. When the French were in control of Vietnam, the street names were French. After their departure and the formation of the new government, only two streets in Saigon kept their former names. They are:

PASTEUR STREET—Named after the famed French scientist and in thanks for the tremendous work accomplished by the Pasteur Institute in Vietnam.

ALEXANDER-DE-RHODES—The French priest who gave the Vietnamese their language in romanized script. (See Chapter 3.)

Streets in Saigon named for Vietnamese heroes include:

TRAN HUNG DAO

The large boulevard connecting Saigon and Cholon bears this famous general's name. In the 13th century his tiny army defeated half a million Mongol invaders, who had already conquered most of Europe and Asia. He subsequently defeated them on two more invasions.

Tran Hung Dao was an uncle of the Emperor Tran Nhan Ton. His nephew made him a hero, and on his death, personally supervised a ten day national funeral for him. His death is a national holiday in South Vietnam today.

LE-LOI

One of the biggest and busiest downtown streets in Saigon is named for a famous leader who for about ten years conducted guerrilla warfare against the Chinese who were ruling the country.

A man of intelligence, Le-Loi had been repeatedly offered Mandarinates by the Chinese but had always refused them. When his forces triumphed against the Chinese, Le-Loi acceded to power as king of Vietnam. He died six years later in 1433 in Hanoi, of beri-beri. While king, he ruled under the name Le-Thai-To.

Vo Tanh

Vo Tanh was a national hero of the 18th century who raised an army with his mother's money, and fought on the side of Nguyen Anh when war was raging between the Nguyen dynasty and the Tay Son. He was extremely successful until 1799 when he was attacked at Qui-Nhon.

He held out against a superior force for two years while hoping for reinforcements from the south. None came and Vo Tanh decided to write to the Tay Son general asking him to spare his troops.

After that, he put on his state dress uniform and assembled his troops around a stake which he had erected in the center of the fort. He told the troops that he had failed in his mission of defending the town, and wished to die at the stake rather than let the enemy see his face. He personally ignited the gunpowder beneath the stake. After his death, Vo Tanh was made a duke by the Emperor Minh Mang and a tomb was built for him in Gia-Dinh province.

Le Van Duyet

An interesting fact about this leader is that he was an eunuch. As in China, the eunuch system was an important institution in Vietnam. When a child was born with a congenital birth defect which would qualify him to become an eunuch, the family had to notify the Court and offer the services of the child. He might be used to guard and supervise the royal harem, or serve as liaison officer between the emperors and the mandarins when he was older. Usually, such a child began his work in the palace at the age of ten or eleven. The family of the child and the entire village from whence he came received tax concessions in compensation.

Some eunuchs won places in the Mandarinate. Besides children born in this condition, others suffering physical injury were also selected, and castration was sometimes used as a recruitment technique.

Le Van Duyet was well liked by the Emperor Gia-Long who unified Vietnam. He was later appointed Governor-General of Saigon by the emperor. Duyet opposed Minh Mang's coming to the throne, but Gia-Long asked him to guide his inexperienced son during the first years of his rule.

Minh Mang, however, detested Le Van Duyet and resented his advice. In 1836, Emperor Minh Mang issued a decree with the purpose of diminishing the power of the eunuchs in government, notably Le Van Duyet. The new regulation forbade eunuchs to interfere in any way with administration and limited them to transmission of orders. He prohibited any more eunuchs from being appointed to the mandarinal corps. This marked the beginning of the end of the eunuch system in Vietnam.

Le Van Duyet was born in 1762 in My Tho near Saigon. After his death, General Le Van Duyet was brought to disgrace when Emperor Minh Mang relieved him posthumously of his rank, and cancelled all nominations and titles conferred on him during his lifetime. He ordered Duyet's tomb to be flattened and surrounded by chains. He also had the tomb symbolically lashed 100 times.

The General's status was restored under later emperors, and a shrine has been erected for him in Gia-Dinh province. (See Chapter 11, places of interest.)

Petrus Ky

Unlucky in politics and diplomacy, Petrus Ky (Truong

Vinh Ky) turned his knowledge of both the East and West to more scholarly applications. He spoke ten languages, was the author of scores of textbooks, and was one of the first newspaper men in Vietnam. Many books from outside Vietnam were translated by Petrus Ky adding immensely to the culture of Vietnam. He died in 1898 at the age of 61 after spending his last years in poverty. Today, he is highly revered and a statue of him is in Saigon. The largest boy's high school and one of the longest avenues in Saigon bear his name.

PHAN THANH GIAN

A self-made Mandarin, who passed the doctorate exam at the age of 29, Phan Thanh Gian is remembered in Vietnam not only as a good administrator, but also a man of letters. He became the country's first Ambassador to a European nation when he went to France in 1858 to negotiate a cease-fire with the French, who had bombarded Da-Nang and taken three of the eastern provinces.

He was considered successful, and the French agreed to move out of the provinces with the exception of a few military bases. The French stipulated that the Vietnamese must pay the costs of supporting the expeditionary forces. A Vietnamese underground did not accept this and rallied support against the invaders. The French marched southward in 1867 to take the southern provinces.

Phan Thanh Gian wanted the Emperor Tu Duc to rally the whole nation against the invaders, but he was not successful in getting the emperor to act. Because he was unable to get a peace treaty with the French, or an agreement to fight them from Emperor Tu Doc, he planned to destroy himself. He went on a hunger strike and as he had not died after two weeks, he took poison on August 4, 1867.

Besides being Vietnam's first Ambassador to France, Phan Thanh Gian was known for his poems and his historical writings, and once served as governor of the southern provinces and devoted himself to developing the area.

When the Vietnamese regained their independence from the French in 1955, a long, narrow, tree-lined street, (where I happened to live in Saigon), was named for Phan Thanh Gian, who told his sons before his death, "Do not collaborate with the French."

CHAPTER

3

THE PEOPLE

General Impressions The first things that newcomers usually notice in Vietnam are the smiling faces of countless children, and the lovely fragile-looking women in their flowing dresses reminiscent of butterflies. The people are a gentle type who are shy, yet can be outgoing with foreigners, especially Americans.

Children love to follow the American men chanting a few words in English, such as, "Hello, GI, you give me candy?" and "You number one." If you don't give the professional child beggars a coin, they will shout, "You number ten." All the while, the children may touch you with their hands and run away, only to creep back again, still smiling. They are intrigued by the hair on American soldiers' arms and often tug at it and giggle.

Families are large in this part of the world, and it is not uncommon to see tiny children lugging around their little brother or sister on their hip. Sometimes the little one may weigh just a few pounds less than his porter; children naturally take care of each other.

Food has been fairly abundant in Vietnam, and you do not see the sadness of hunger on children's faces except in extreme cases. They seem almost fearless and fun-loving. An example of this was clearly shown during the 1963 coup d'etat in Saigon when youngsters went right behind tanks and soldiers firing guns, picking up empty shell casings.

Dress The women of Vietnam have, in my opinion, one of the most beautiful national costumes in the world. It is called the "ao-dai." The over-dress is form-fitting to the waist, with long tight sleeves. At the waist, two panels extend front and back to cover the long satin trousers underneath. Correct fit dictates that the pants reach the sole of the foot, and are always slightly longer than the dress panels. Occasionally lace is sewn around the bottom of each leg. Tradition has kept the color of the pants of the ao-dai to black or white.

The traditional ao-dai has a high mandarian collar and is favored by most of the Vietnamese men for their wives and other family members, as well as their girl friends. Young moderns, however, often choose the newer "Madame Nhu" or boat neckline which is far more comfortable in the tropical heat. After the coup d'etat of 1963 when the Diem regime was deposed, it was rumored that this style ao-dai would be banned, but so far nothing has happened.

The dress portion of the ao-dai is often made of nylon and comes in a variety of bright colors and designs. The extremely dressy ao-dai is usually made from brocade or elaborately embroidered material.

When a woman sits down, she takes the back panel, pulls it up and around into her lap. When riding a bicycle, they often tie the back panel down to the back fender to keep it from getting tangled in the wheels. Often, girls can be seen riding along the streets of Saigon on motor bikes with the back of their ao-dai flying loose, causing foreigners to comment that they look like butterflies, and beautiful ones at that.

Many Americans have become so fond of the dress that they have some specially made to send home to their families. They make excellent hostess gowns.

Many of the Vietnamese wear plain black satin trousers with a short shirt for their everyday work.

In addition to these, one sees a variety of Chinese and Western-type dresses worn in Vietnam. The Vietnamese male however, generally objects to women wearing Western clothing.

The men have a costume that has been almost completely replaced by Western dress in Vietnam today. It is similar to the ao-dai, except the outer garment is shorter and not tightly fitted. They are usually worn by older men or in traditional ceremonies.

Children generally wear Western-type dress until they are teenagers. Little girls may occasionally be seen in the ao-dai on special occasions.

Womens' Hairstyles Generally, Vietnamese women wear their hair quite long. It is usually very healthy looking, jet-black, and rather fine in texture. Those who can afford it will spend many hours in beauty shops having their hair done in elaborate styles, often upswept. Others will wear it hanging loosely down their back. Older women from the south have traditionally worn their hair pulled back to the nape of their neck and rolled into a bun. Those of the north wear theirs in a roll pulled across the top of the head.

Vietnamese Diet The Vietnamese is normally much smaller in stature than an average American, with many women weighing under 100 pounds and men weighing between 115 and 135 pounds.

In one day, a Vietnamese will consume only about two-thirds the calories that an American would, but the caloric intake per capita of 2,490 per day ranks among the highest in Asia.

Rice is the staple food. Other foods preferred are fish, pork, various soups laden with noodles, tongue, heart, stomach and a variety of intestines, coagulated blood from animals, spices, hot peppers, a pungent fish sauce called "nuoc-mam," soy-bean sauces, vegetables, fresh fruits, and green tea.

One of the most popular foods is the soup called "Pho" which is sold everywhere on the streets. Pho is the Vietnamese snack, and is eaten for breakfast, lunch, dinner, and anytime in between. The Americans have nick-named the mobile soup kitchens "Howard Johnson's."

Fruits and vegetables from Dalat are wonderful and usually are of prime quality.

Sweets are made from rice glutine, fruits, seed, and spices. Coconut cakes are very popular. Children love to be given

American candy. If an American starts giving out candy to his little Vietnamese friends on the street, he should be prepared to continue the practice and not mind having hundreds of kids following him around. Chinese food is also popular.

VIETNAMESE SOCIETY

VIETNAMESE society can be generally classified so that the foreigner can more readily understand the people with whom he might come in contact.

The most important group in Vietnam, in my opinion, is the plain ordinary people, often heard called "peasants." I wish we had a nicer term to denote these fine, long-suffering people. They are very curious about life outside of their own areas and are generally friendly. They are known for their patience and have suffered greatly in the numerous conflicts in the country. They are often the victims of circumstance and of disease. Because of their numbers, they do most of the back-breaking work. These poor people are the backbone of Vietnam and are the main ones about whom this book is written. They may well be the ones who will determine the outcome of the present conflict in Vietnam.

One group which has a limited understanding of Americans and other foreigners and their way of life, and little opportunity to find out, is the working class from the urban and rural areas. People falling into this grouping might be the shopkeeper, low-level civil servant, businessmen, average white collar workers, skilled workers, etc. A lack of understanding of customs and culture both on the part of the

Vietnamese and the Americans has occasionally caused friction between the two groups. Better understanding is particularly desired with these people.

Another group might be represented by employees of Vietnamese governmental agencies and private companies. Many of these employees have been greatly influenced by French culture, and most of them speak fluent French, having been educated in French schools in Vietnam or France. Their views of Americans are oftentimes influenced by this French culture and by U.S. movies shown in Vietnam. These people are often leaders in their communities and politically powerful. They are on occasion especially critical of Americans and their culture.

There is also a group of Vietnamese who are quite progressive and change to whatever is in vogue at the moment, and a considerable number of them hold citizenships other than Vietnamese. They are usually quite studious and will make every effort to learn whatever is required to be up to date. Westerners have traditionally mixed easily with this group, as they are anxious to learn Western customs and culture.

Many Vietnamese are working with the Americans either directly in American installations or in Vietnamese governmental positions. They have often been to school outside Vietnam, perhaps in the United States. They understand the Western way of life much better than most Vietnamese and provide an important entree for Americans into Vietnamese culture. However, Americans should not be led to believe that these are traditional Vietnamese. Often, they have become so westernized that they are a class apart from their fellow countrymen. There are those, of course, who have maintained their Vietnamese way of life.

People following Confucian ethics and traditional culture are still greatly in evidence in Vietnam and make up another grouping. They should be handled with all due respect. They sometimes believe that foreigners place too much emphasis on materialism. These people are often the unspoken leaders of small communities and are well respected by their neighbors and friends.

IMPORTANT ETHNIC GROUPS

THERE ARE four main categories of minority groups in South Vietnam. They are the Montagnards, Chinese, Cambodians and Chams. In North Vietnam, the most important are the Montagnards or mountain people, made up of the Thai, Muong, Mans, Lolos, and Meo tribes. The Montagnards are said to number over two million in the north. In the south, the figures show approximately one million Montagnards, one million Chinese, 400,000 Cambodians, and 20,000 Chams. These ethnic minorities represent approximately 15 per cent of the population of the two Vietnams.

In the south, the two most important groups are the Chinese and the Montagnards. The Cambodians whose land was conquered years ago by the Vietnamese have virtually been absorbed into the Vietnamese community. They have inter-married, shared the same religions, customs, and culture. The Chams are such a small group that they hold little significance in the political structure of South Vietnam. Also, they are so closely related to the Montagnards that they are often considered one of their sub-groups.

The Chinese

Even though the majority of the Chinese in Vietnam were born there, they consider themselves "Chinese" and not Vietnamese. They have been the successful businessmen traditionally. Prejudice between Chinese and Vietnamese has existed for years.

In 1956, the government of South Vietnam issued orders making Chinese born in Vietnam, into Vietnamese citizens. Chinese not accepting Vietnamese citizenship were also barred from a group of occupations that had been primarily held by Chinese in the country. The Chinese retaliated by drawing large sums of money from the banks in Vietnam, and boycotting the purchase of Vietnamese rice for sale in their stores. Their action had a temporary effect of lowering the value of the *piastre* in the money markets of Hong Kong and Singapore.

The government persisted, however, and eventually a large number of Chinese in the country assumed Vietnamese citizenship. Those not doing so paid yearly fees for maintaining their foreign passports. As for being denied the privilege of doing business in certain fields unless they were citizens, they merely turned over the signing of papers to a relative who was a Vietnamese citizen, thus skirting the law.

The Chinese schools were also placed under government control and teachers were forbidden to wear Chinese dress. The Vietnamese flag and national anthem were given honors daily and the Vietnamese language was made a requirement in the curriculum.

Today, the majority of the Chinese in South Vietnam have segregated themselves into one area known as Cholon, an adjoining city to Saigon. In the past, very few Chinese, even though citizens, were drafted into the Army. Latest information from Vietnam now indicates that some of them are being drafted at this time.

The Chinese are still the shrewd businessmen in Vietnam, as they are in many of the countries around the world.

Their customs and culture vary little from that of the Vietnamese. In fact, many of the Vietnamese customs have come directly from the Chinese who dominated the country for so many years.

The Montagnards Other names for the Montagnards (which is French for mountaineers) includes "highlanders"; "tribespeople"; and "moi." The term "moi" is disliked by the mountain people because roughly translated the word means "savages." Officially, the South Vietnamese government now calls the Montagnards "Dong-Bao-Thouong" which means "Compatriots of the Highlands."

The land inhabited by the Montagnards is also called by different names; the Highlands, the Annamite Chain, or the Plateau de Montagnards.

The history of these people is confused and disintegrated. It is believed that they descended from a mixture of Indonesians, Australian aborigines, Negroid Panpans of Melanesia, and other Pacific island races.

The mountain people of Vietnam are very different from the ethnic Vietnamese. Not only is their appearance at variance, their customs and culture vary considerably. Their language is entirely different. A lengthy study could be written on the Montagnards alone.

In the Appendices of this book, a comprehensive listing of the tribes of North and South Vietnam is included with estimated population figures, location, and pertinent facts, available. General impressions of the Montagnards are included here to give the reader an idea of what their life is like.

LANGUAGE Each tribe may speak a different language and individuals must resort to sign language to communicate. The tribes can generally be divided into two groups according to the type language they speak—Mon-Khmer or Malayo-Polynesian. The Mon-Khmer languages are used by many small groups living in different parts of Southeast Asia. Malayo-Polynesian languages are used in some parts of Indonesia and different islands in the Pacific. The tribes that use the Malayo-Polynesian languages in Vietnam include the Jarai, Hroi, Raday, Raglai, Chru, and Cham. It is believed that they are the most recent arrivals to Vietnam among the mountain people. They have probably been in the area no more than 3,000 years.

Another linguistic division that may apply to the northern mountain people includes dialects of Tibeto-Chinese origin.

GENERAL IMPRESSIONS The Montagnards have been treated poorly in the past by their Vietnamese contemporaries. They have had little opportunity for schooling or occupational training. As a group, they are poor farmers with primitive, outdated methods.

Their whole lives, except for the Christian converts, are ruled by spirits and fear. A simple thing such as a crow alighting on a house being built, is considered to be a bad omen, and all work on that house is ended forever.

Missionaries, American Special Forces and members of the US Aid Program have taken the most interest in the mountain people. Americans are generally well-liked by the Montagnards and it might be added that the reverse is also true. Most Americans who have worked and lived in the Montagnard areas have found the people to be interesting, loyal, good fighters, and just plain "good people."

The Jarai Tribe of South Vietnam Since there are so many tribes and customs, one fairly representative tribe is chosen here to give the reader a better understanding of the Montagnards.

The Jarai have a matrilineal kinship system. The groom goes to the wife's home, takes her name and must never joke with his mother-in-law! Daughters inherit the wordly goods, which always belong to the wife. It should be noted that different tribes have different kinship systems, a few of which are like those of the United States.

The Jarai consider moving their home when they have exhausted the resources of the land where they are living. They fall into the category of being semi-nomadic. They will move their homes more often should a catastrophe take place in the village, such as an epidemic, visits by tigers, or if lightning strikes the village, etc.

Animals such as water buffaloes, horses, and goats are raised for their meat, and are often sacrificed during ceremonies. Chickens and dogs are always present, and many people raise pigs.

Magico-religious factors are used in selecting land for farming, and burning is the method of clearing land for cultivation.

The basic diet of the Jarai consists of rice, maize, vegetables, beef, buffalo, pork, chicken, goat, snake, turtles, rats, and sometimes dog. Fish is eaten when available. Meat from cattle is usually eaten during celebrations.

Animals are speared and killed in special ceremonies, and the animal's carcass, hide, and all, is thrown on the fire. The people soon begin to cut the meat and it is eaten practically raw. The intestines are regarded as a delicacy, as well as chopped raw meat mixed with fresh animal blood.

The Jarai eat rice and boiled vegetables twice daily and they eat with their fingers.

Many people are addicted to alcohol and even little children drink rice wine. Sometimes, the whole population can be found in drunken stupors at times of celebrations. In some villages, people have been without rice for food because it has been used to make alcohol.

Men, women, and often children smoke tobacco rolled in banana leaves.

Many women are bare-breasted but some become shy in the presence of foreigners and are wearing more clothing. The men wear loin cloths.

Homes are built on stilts, four to five feet off the ground. They are called long-houses and are long and narrow. Floors and walls are made of bamboo and roofs are thatched. The people sleep on straw mats on the floor.

The Jarai believe accidents and diseases are caused by spirits and that sorcerers can cause all kinds of bad happenings, including death. They think that if they violate taboos, the whole village can be brought to suffering. Some of the punishments might be a lack of rain, epidemics, etc. Sacrifices must be made to placate the spirits and bring things back to normal. The village sorcerer is often called in to determine which spirit has been offended.

It is interesting to note that a sorcerer from a Vietnamese tribe has been converted to the Christian faith by the Christian and Missionary Alliance personnel.

Their religion is also surrounded by superstition. Elements of nature are considered to be manifestations of the various spirits or gods. They have gods and goddesses of sky, water, mountains, trees, rocks, etc.

There are no special churches, but sacrifices and ceremonies can be practiced at any given time or place. All important occasions are postponed until an appropriate sacrifice can be made to the spirits and gods.

THE VIETNAMESE LANGUAGE

AUTHORITIES do not seem to completely agree on the origin of the Vietnamese language. German linguists have said that they believe the Vietnamese language belongs to the Pegouan, Thai, or Mon-Khmer group. Some believe it is of Thai origin while another expert, Reverend Father Souvignet, traced it to the Indo-Malay group. Still another dissenter, A. G. Haudricourt, wrote that he believed it could more properly be placed in the Austro-Asiatic family of languages. Nguyen-Dinh-Hoa of Saigon's Faculty of Letters has said that the Vietnamese lexicon has many nouns in common with the Cambodian or Khmer language. This is especially true of nouns dealing with parts of the body, members of the kinship system, names of farm tools, species of flora and fauna, etc. He also added that Vietnamese used many of the same final consonants as Thai and used various levels of pitch and tone.

New words have also been added into the Vietnamese

language during the times of Chinese domination and other outside influences in the country, such as French and American. Most of the words derived from these languages have been "Vietnamized" and given their own pronunciations.

The Vietnamese used Chinese characters or Chu Nho (scholars script) as their written language vehicle beginning in the ninth century. The Chinese characters came into use in all official transactions, correspondence, and literature. No one can reliably say what written language was used prior to this time in Vietnam.

The written Chinese language, Chu Nho, was different from the spoken Vietnamese. Citizens of various countries of the Asian world could write to each other and be understood. They did not pronounce the characters the same way, however, and could not expect to understand a conversation, should they have met.

Vietnamese scholars and literary types demanded history and literature in a language of their own, and started to borrow Chinese characters, improvising their own combinations to represent ideas and concepts, and to phonetize some of their native speech. This became known as " Chu Nom" which meant vulgar or demotic script. It looks like Chinese, but no foreigners could read it, as they could with Chu Nho. Chu Nom was found only in literary works, unofficial documents and the like.

During the seventeenth century, Catholic missionaries began to arrive in Vietnam from Spain, Portugal, Italy, and France. They needed some linguistic tool to get their ideas across to the people. Under the guidance of the Catholic Priest, Father Alexander-de-Rhodes, a system of romanized writing, known as "Quoc Ngu" (national language) was developed. This enabled them to use the spoken Vietnamese in a written manner through the Roman alphabet. Father Alexander-de-Rhodes completed a Vietnamese-Portuguese-Latin dictionary in 1649. He was a Jesuit scholar-missionary from France who studied in Vietnam for twelve years under another Jesuit, Francisco de Pina, before compiling the new written language.

In 1920, Quoc-Ngu was recognized as the official language. Since 1945, Quoc-Ngu has been used in all lower level schools in Vietnam. There has been considerable controversy about using the national language at the university level, replacing French. On several occasions, especially at times of poor Vietnamese-French relations, students have demonstrated in behalf of using Vietnamese entirely in the university curriculum.

Technicalities of the Language The Vietnamese language is far too complicated to be throughly treated in a book of this type. For information purposes only, however, a few of the characteristics of the language follow.

There are 12 vowels and 27 consonants in the language. It is a tonal language, and a given syllable may be pronounced in any of six tones. A classic example is the word "ma." Depending on the voice inflection given the word, it can mean ghost, cheek, but grave, horse, or rice-seedling. There may also be other meanings, depending on the melody of the given sentence.

The language is noted for its lack of inflectional endings

or the changing of form of the word to indicate number, gender, etc. Translated to English, a Vietnamese sentence and might read:

"Today John give I six pencil."

Modifiers always follow the noun, adjective, verb, or adverb that they modify. Many words are left out. One might compare a Vietnamese sentence with a thrifty telegram; all words that can be left out are omitted. It may have an understood subject or no subject at all.

The numerical system is decimal.

In the Appendices of this book may be found selected elements of the basic Vietnamese language; alphabet; glossary of selected vocabulary; and useful phrases.

CHAPTER

4

RELIGIONS

RELIGION has played an important role in present day history in Vietnam. President Ngo Dinh Diem's government was toppled after a long seige of activity by Buddhists, who claimed religious discrimination on the part of the Catholic President, his family, and their government. In the past, many religious groups have had armies of their own.

Despite all of this, there is little evidence of religious conflict between the people on a day-to-day basis. Everyone seems to go his own way in this respect, as shown by the numerous religions in practice in the country today. Often, an individual's religion is a combination of many different beliefs.

There is no religious belief in South Vietnam which is recognized as the official religion of the government. Leaders of the nation have generally been from different religious faiths.

Basically, the Vietnamese are a very religious people, and

this is the reason for the numerous pagodas and temples in the country. Many of them have been built and dedicated to famous people who have served Vietnam, including national heroes, craftsmen (see Chapter 7), and other men of virtue and religion.

The majority of the religions discussed are also practiced in North Vietnam. Many Catholics fled the north in 1955 when the country was divided, because they were afraid of religious persecution under the communists.

CONFUCIANISM

Origin Confucianism began in China in the sixth century B.C. Confucius, a scholar and "ne'er do well" politician, was a contemporary of Buddha and Pythagoras. He believed that he was divinely inspired to show the correct way of life to his fellow men.

Therefore, Confucianism is not truly a religion, but is a way of life involving a code of ethics and morals. It was introduced into Vietnam at the beginning of the Chinese domination during the first centuries of the Christian era. Even after the Chinese were pushed out of Vietnam, their influence of Confucianism remained with the people.

Growth Since Confucianism is not an organized religion, there are no figures as to the number of followers it has in Vietnam. However, Confucianism has a tremendous influence on the life of the Vietnamese people. Many practice it and belong to other religions. It is considered practical for the rich and the poor alike.

Beliefs Confucius did not believe in a supreme being, but believed in "force" and "matter." He believed that man was essentially of a good nature, but that he must constantly work to keep it. He taught conscience and that man could distinguish between good and evil. By adhering to virtue, one would receive tranquility of the soul.

Confucius accepted the main religious rites, but rejected many superstitions and the idea of eternal life via reincarnation as believed by the Hindus of that time. He taught that man was made up of a living and spiritual soul. At death, the living soul turned to dust along with the body, but the spiritual soul wanders in the ethereal realm. He taught that this spiritual soul could evaporate into nothing; therefore, it was the duty of living persons, through ancestor worship, to keep the spiritual soul alive. He also believed in the enjoyment of a simple life with harmony in social relations.

As a scholar, Confucius compiled the classics from the Chou period in Chinese history (1100–481 B.C.). These books became a standard of Confucian orthodoxy.

Besides Confucian ethics, regulations involving relationships between people, such as emperor and subjects; fathers and sons; husbands and wives; elderly and young etc. were prescribed. Confucius believed that harmony could only be achieved by obeying these laws. Only by achieving harmony can one have tranquility of the soul.

In order to conform to these principles and ensure harmony, Confucius said that one must follow a group of high moral principles of relationship which were called "Phan" and to observe rules of etiquette and ritual, called "Li," which were in the books he compiled.

One of the rules in Confucius's books was similar to the Golden Rule in the Christian Bible and yet it appeared long before the birth of Christ. It said, "What you do not want done to yourself, do not do to others."

Under Confucianism, a man maintains an even temper; shows himself as being just and fair; adjusts to the life around him; avoids exaggeration and practices ancestor worship.

Perhaps the most important feature of Confucianism regards the family. In the system, the father is highly respected and completely rules the family and the household. The rest of the family practices filial piety. Confucius emphasized that his beliefs should be taught by example, thus in the right Confucian manner, the father would rule with a stern, but loving, and compassionate hand.

Ritual The most important ritual in Confucianism is that of ancestor worship.

Most Vietnamese homes will have an altar dedicated to the family ancestors. It will be decorated with candlesticks, incense bowls, flower trays, an alcohol pot, and the tablet containing the names of those ancestors who have died during the past five generations.

On the anniversary of each ancestor's death, offerings of food and symbolic votive paper, clothes, money, houses, etc. are made by the chief of the family. The chief of the family varies in Vietnam according to the area. In some areas, the oldest son is chief. In others, it is the youngest son. Prayers are said to all the ancestors and then to the ancestor whose anniversary is being celebrated. He is asked to return and receive the offerings. Even though the more modern Vietnamese know that the ancestor probably doesn't receive the gifts, they do this out of respect.

In addition to the anniversary veneration, ancestors are worshipped on other special days including festivals and holidays. Other opportunities to pay homage to them are at major family events such as weddings, graduations, births, etc. These are held to apprise the ancestors of family events. Far more elaborate preparations and more ceremonies are held for a period of two years after a death. (See Chapter 6.)

In the Confucian theory of filial piety, ancestor worship is extremely important. After parents die, they must be venerated in such a way as to testify to the children's gratitude and to ask for protection and blessings from their souls.

They believe that the deceased ancestors can continue to play a role in their children's lives, sharing the family's joys and sorrows. The souls of the departed ancestors warn their descendents through dreams about misfortunes which can be avoided.

In addition to the altar at home, family clans often have ancestral halls where the tablets containing the names of the oldest ancestors are kept. Sometimes, this place is the home of the chief of the clan. Each clan is a unit of Vietnamese society extending to nine generations. The chief of the clan is responsible for carrying out the veneration of the ancestors. He pays for all the expenses of the ceremony and receives the use of the clan's property in compensation. Sometimes, relatives may bring symbolic gifts to help out on this occasion. Often dinners are held on these occasions.

Thus, with ancestor veneration, the Vietnamese family

demonstrates to their children the virtues of filial obedience, piety, and family continuity. This is the bond that binds the family so closely together and continues ties with the dead.

A family that does not have sons to continue this ancestor veneration is thought to have received the worst fate dealt to mankind. They will often adopt a son and leave him money to continue the veneration ceremonies. A family that has no son to continue this process is thought to have "disappeared" forever.

Any failure in fulfilling filial duty is considered to be a crime, and it is every family member's obligation to try and earn fame and wealth to increase his clan's reputation and to please the ancestors.

CAO DAI

Origin In 1921, Mr. Ngo Van Chieu was the Chief of Phu Quoc island off the coast of Ha Tien province. To pass the lonely evenings, he went to seances. One evening at a seance, a spirit told him that he was to found the Cao Dai religion and would worship an "all-seeing eye," and to follow a vegetarian diet for three years. Four years later, Chieu went to Saigon and began to attract followers to the new religion. Later, two followers of the religion, Le Van Trung and Pham Cong Tac took over much of its leadership when Chieu went to Can Tho to establish a new branch of the sect.

Growth Le Van Trung's organizational efforts resulted in over 20,000 followers within a year. The religion rapidly spread until it had three million followers. The reason for its popularity may be that it combines many different religions, appealing to the Vietnamese who have been exposed to them all.

Beliefs Cao Dai believe that the God of Christians and Jews, is also the Supreme Being of the Buddhists, and the Brahmnan of the Hindu. They contend that different religions were founded because of a lack of communication and transportation, and that all religions are seeds of wisdom planted by God.

The founder, Nguyen Van Chieu said that there were three amnesties of sin granted by God. The first was proclaimed through Moses and Jesus; the second through Buddha and Lao-Tse; and the third was delivered through spiritualistic seances. He claimed that he received the third, but would not be the last to receive the divine messages.

Cao Dai morality believes in man's duty to himself, his family, society, and humanity. Its members should seek pure spirituality without seeking honor and riches. Some of these beliefs can be traced to other religions. For instance, Confucianism teaches obligations to society and ancestor veneration; Buddhism teaches reincarnation and not eating meat. Taoism discourages honor and riches. The church is organized along similar lines as those of the Catholic church and has a Western type political structure.

The Cao Dai also believe in spirits, eternal life after death, heaven and hell, and ancestor worship.

Requirements of followers differ with their category: special clergy, clergy, and laymen. For example, a layman should follow a vegetarian diet six days a month, fast regularly, and follow the commandments. These requirements are more stringent for the clergy. The commandments include prohibitions against killing living creatures, stealing, eating meat, drinking alcohol excessively, sinful sexual intercourse, and lying.

Places of Worship and Ritual There are numerous Cao Dai temples in Vietnam, but the largest and most impressive one is at Tay-Ninh, 55 miles northwest of Saigon. It looks like a cathedral on the outside and is rather unusual inside. The ceiling is extremely high similar to many Catholic cathedrals. Inside there are odd-looking statues of Confucius, Jesus, Buddha, Lao-Tse, Brahman, Siva, and Vishnu. There are pictures of their "spiritual guides" who include Victor Hugo, the French writer and poet; Sun Yat Sen, the founder of the Chinese Nationalist Republic; and Trang Trinh, a Vietnamese diviner.

The Cao Dai also claim to have spiritual contact with Shakespeare and intend to establish contact with Churchill.

The triangle is a sign of the Cao Dai. It represents Sun Yat Sen, Trang Trinh, and Victor Hugo (as described above) and surrounds the all-seeing eye of God in the middle.

There are four prayer times each day. Laymen should pray at the most convenient time to them. At the midnight prayer time, however, Cao Dai, their God, speaks to the people through a medium.

Priests in the Cao Dai wear different color robes according to the branch in which they belong: Confucian—red; Taoist—sky blue; Buddhist—saffron. The Superior wears white with trim of the three colors representing the branches.

Women may become members of the clergy but must always wear white. They may rise to the rank of Cardinal.

Political and Military Background This religious sect had an army of its own and wielded a lot of power. They were encouraged by the French to establish physical control over the provinces in which they were numerous, after the Japanese withdrawal. This was a means to fight communism that was filling the vacuum when the Japanese left. By 1950, the sect ran their provinces like an autonomous state with troops.

In 1955, the new South Vietnamese government, led by President Diem, told them to lay down their arms and revert to their former religious status. A few were eliminated by force. Their leader, Pham Con Tac, fled to Cambodia taking some church funds with him. He died in 1963.

After the coup d'etat in November 1963, the church resumed its religious activities on a fairly large scale. The new leader is Tran Quang Vinh of Tay Ninh.

BUDDHISM

Origin Buddhism was originated in India about 500 B.C. by Gautama Buddha and was carried to other Asian and Far-Eastern countries. It reached Vietnam as early as A.D. 189 when Chinese bonzes took refuge in North Vietnam during a period of dissention in China, following the death of the Chinese Emperor Han Linh De. In the third century, more bonzes came to Vietnam, this time from India.

Growth The history of Vietnam's Buddhism can be classified into four stages: the beginning, the height of its glory, a period of decline, and a period of revival.

The beginning is characterized by the first bonzes coming into Vietnam from China and India, spreading the first knowledge about Buddhism among the Vietnamese people. This epoch can be placed between the second and the sixth centuries, B.C.

The period in which Buddhism reached its height in the country was between the seventh and the fourteenth centuries, A.D. During this time, the kings of Vietnam were especially interested in Buddhism and made it the religion of the kingdom. They often donned the habit of bonzes themselves and had many pagodas built in the country. The kings conferred the title of Master of the Kingdom on the Superior of the Buddhist clergy. The kings of this period are often quoted by historians as having been very devoted to the welfare of the people and as having led exemplary lives.

Buddhism began to decline in the sixteenth century during the last part of the Le Dynasty. The kings lost interest in the religion; the bonzes became less learned and began to turn away from the original form of Buddhism and substituted many practices that were considered to be little more than superstition. Also, Buddhism was verbally attacked by the scholars of the Confucianist school.

Buddhism, nevertheless, remained an important part of the religious life of the people of Vietnam.

During the French administration of Vietnam, some restrictions were placed on the Buddhists, such as limitation on the number of monks per pagoda; no new pagodas could be constructed without prior French approval; and limitations were set on the acceptance of gifts and legacies.

According to a Vietnamese writer, this caused the more scholarly and devout Buddhists to withdraw from active participation in Buddhist affairs. As a result, those who employed more mysticism, tantrism, animism, and polytheism, became more active in the religion.

In 1920, an attempt was made to reform the Buddhist religion in Vietnam. Those working with this called it "restoring" Buddhism, and attempted to eliminate non-Buddhist elements of belief and practice from the religion in Vietnam at the time.

The Associations for Buddhist Studies were established in Saigon in 1931; in Hue in 1932; and in Hanoi in 1934. An attempt was made to strengthen discipline in the monasteries, improve the religious training for priests and to change the written vehicle of Buddhism in Vietnam from Chinese to the newer romanized Vietnamese. As this was still during the French control of the country, it was evidently done with their blessing.

Some of the Buddhist activities were slowed down during the years of World War II and the French-Viet-Minh war. Major works continued, however.

In 1949, a wave of rehabilitation and new building began among the Buddhist organizations in Hanoi and Hue. Buddhist periodicals began to be published again, and authors and translators took up their work once more.

A new Association for Buddhist Studies was begun in 1951 in Saigon as the older one had become ineffective.

A Buddhist National Congress convened at Hue in 1951

and voted the unification of the three associations of Hanoi, Hue, and Saigon. Plans were laid by the congress for the increased propagation of the religion to include the formation of a Buddhist Youth Movement and joining the World Buddhist Fellowship.

Later, when a Buddhist relic enroute to the World Congress meeting in Tokyo was allowed to stay in Saigon for 24 hours, a solemn reception drew more than fifty thousand Buddhists to the scene, with less than six day's notice. This successful gathering was said to have re-invigorated Buddhism throughout Vietnam.

The 1954 partition of Vietnam ended relationships between the northern Buddhists and the two southern units.

Buddhism Today Buddhism emerged as a powerful political force in South Vietnam after a series of repressions from the government of the late President Diem. They brought world attention to Vietnam when the Venerable Thich Quang Duc burned himself to death at the intersection of Le Van Duyet and Phan Ding Phung streets in Saigon at approximately 9 a.m. on June 11, 1963, in protest against the Diem regime. This event was memorably photographed by the outstanding Associated Press Correspondent, Malcome Browne and within hours his pictures flashed around the world. Several other Buddhist clergy members followed suit, but none in so spectacular a manner.

Compared with Buddhism in other Asian countries, the religion does not seem as well organized in Vietnam. Of course, many of these other countries have offered state support to the religion. The pagodas are not nearly so elaborate in Vietnam as those found in other Asian countries.

To the casual onlooker, Buddhism appears to be most appealing to the women of the country, and the young people and men do not seem to take as much interest in the religion as their counterparts in other Asian countries.

It has been estimated that there are approximately 10 million fervent Buddhists in North and South Vietnam with approximately another 40% of the remaining population being nominal followers. There are approximately 30–33 million people in North and South Vietnam.

There are those who contend that at least 95% of the southern country is Buddhist and cite as examples the large number of followers involved in the demonstrations, riots and other public gatherings before and after the Diem regime was toppled. It is my opinion that the old saying, "all the world loves a parade" would be a more apt explanation of the numbers in the numerous demonstrations in the country. The history of Buddhism in Vietnam clearly shows that it is not nearly so strong there as it is in other Asian countries.

Beliefs There are two major branches of Buddhism. One is called Mahayana, the Greater Vehicle. The second is named Hinayana, the Lesser Vehicle. The Mahayana is practiced in southern areas. This is the state religion of the Cambodians. Also, the large Cambodian minority group in Vietnam live in the southern delta area.

THE MAHAYANA (Greater Vehicle)

The doctrine was developed in India during the first and second centuries after the Birth of Christ. This division of Buddhism is primarily practiced in the countries of Chinese civilization such as China, Tibet, Korea, and Vietnam.

This group considers Gautama Buddha as one of many "Enlightened Ones" or Buddhas and a divine manifestation of the god of the universe. They believe that anyone could become a Buddha, but there are very few people who have actually attained Buddhahood. Those who try to become a Buddha by living lives of perfection according to the Buddhist doctrine are called "bodhisatvas."

They believe that man must save others before he can be saved himself and that love must be expressed through compassion and good works. The priests of the Mahayana branch are bodhisatvas who live in a community and help others attain salvation.

THE HINAYANA DIVISION (Lesser Vehicle)

Started about the fourth century after the birth of Christ, it has kept closer to Buddhist orthodoxy than the other branches. Their scriptures are written in Pali.

It is primarily practiced in countries along the Indian Ocean, Ceylon, Thailand, Burma, Cambodia, Laos, and the southern delta of South Vietnam.

Youngsters following this belief retire for a short period into Buddhist monasteries as student monks, called "arhats." They do not take any binding vows which cannot be revoked and may leave when they so desire. Like the monk, the arhat's possessions are few, limited to the necessities of a saffron robe, begging bowl, water strainer, needle, and razor.

The Hinayana branch followers believe that Buddha was not a diety but was just a man who was a good teacher and master. Therefore, one may venerate Buddha if he so desires, but it is not necessary for salvation. According to their belief, one can reach Nirvana during life on earth,

Gautama Buddha and His Teachings

Buddha was a prince of the Sakya clan in India and lived in the fifth century B.C. He married at an early age, 16, and later had a son. One account states that he had three wives.

Buddha was distressed at the sights he saw outside of his own private world living as a prince. Finally, he left home at the age of 29 to seek new answers for the problems he saw. He was especially unhappy with the Brahman teaching of reincarnation or one soul being transmitted from body to body in an eternal never ending existence. He felt that this was one of the prime causes of the misery he saw, and he sought an escape.

He sought out the priests of the day and talked with them but was not satisfied. He and five friends decided to take up asceticism, and they almost starved themselves to death. This did not provide any satisfaction either, and only left them weak and ill.

Six years later, Buddha sat under a Pippala Banyan (Bodhi) tree and made up his mind that he would stay there until he found a solution. The answer supposedly came to him after 49 days, and he sought to spread the word to others through his teachings.

Among the things he preached are the following concepts:

Moderation and the middle path were emphasized.

Self-denial is as bad as over-indulgence.

Four noble truths were taught: life is a succession of suffering; ignorance of true reality is the cause of suffering; by eliminating selfish desires man can eliminate suffering; man must strive to perfect himself through right concentration, speech, action, and living.

Reincarnation is basic to the belief. Everyone has had

many previous lives and will have future lives. A record is kept of the sum total of one's good and bad actions during these lives. This is called the law of Karma. At the end of a life, if the good actions outnumber the bad ones, the future life will be better. If not, the next life will be worse. This accounts for the Buddhist fear of killing animals and insects, as well as that of killing people.

After living many lives, with a good Karma, one may enter Nirvana, a state of oneness with the universe—a point at which the endless cycle of reincarnations is ended. Peace of the soul is thus attained.

HOA HAO

Origin The Hoa Hao religious sect gets its name from a village in the That Son mountain range of An Giang province. This village is the birthplace of Huynh Phu So, the founder of the religion.

Huynh Phu So was a sickly boy in his youth and his father entrusted his care to a monk who was considered to be a healer. His name was Thay Xom, but he was known as Monk Tra Son because he practiced medicine and religion in a place by that name. Monk Tra Son was a disciple of a philosopher by the name of Nguyen Van Huyen who lived on Mount Cam in the mountain range. He often came down from his home to teach the villagers about self-denial, spiritual discipline, and Buddhism. Thus, Huyuh Phu So is also considered to be a student of Nguyen Van Huyen.

The Monk Tra Son was never able to cure Huynh Phu So, but the young man continued to live with him until the monk died. He then returned to his home. In 1930, he was supposed to have arisen from his bed one night and prostrated himself before the family ancestral altar. From that day on, he was cured and declared himself a prophet and began to preach.

Growth Huynh Phu So was known as a fantastic miracle "healer" and was so dynamic that he had over 100,000 followers within one year. He was called the "living Buddha." The number of followers eventually grew to almost two million. At the present time, the religion does not have such a large following, due to political and military movements. It is strongest in An Giang province.

Beliefs This religion is considered to be the poor man's dream. It is an offshoot of Buddhism without all the expense of that religion.

Huynh Phu So's teachings included the following:

Elaborate pagodas were unnecessary. There was also no necessity for fancy rituals or large numbers of priests in order to worship God.

Internal faith is more important than external experiences or ceremonies. In essence, he said, "It is better to pray with a pure heart before the family altar than to perform a lot of gaudy ceremonies in a pagoda with an evil heart."

Offerings were approved of for Buddha, one's ancestors, and for national heroes, but not for other spirits.

Elaborate and costly funerals which caused great impoverishment for the living were not desirable. Mr. So taught that it was better to do good things for people while they were living than after they died.

Ritual Followers of the religion pray four times each day. The prayers are for Buddha, the Reign of the Enlightened King, ancestors—living and dead, and for the masses of little people. Each group is prayed for at a separate session.

Prayers are said before a simple table covered with a plain red cloth with four characters inscribed upon it: "Bao Son Ky Huong," a good scent from a strange mountain. Water and flowers are offered instead of wine and food. Incense is used to ward off evil spirits.

There is a Hoa Hao shrine located in An Giang province near Long Xuyen at Tan Chau village.

Political and Military Background This sect was important militarily and politically with the French, the Japanese, and the succeeding governments led by Diem and those that overthrew his government.

The leader of the sect, Huynh Phu So, had so many followers before and during the Second World War that the French became concerned. He was arrested and placed in a mental hospital for almost a year.

At this time, the Japanese were streaming into Vietnam, and became interested in the religious sects as a means to establish anti-French forces. They armed the Hoa Hao and promised to grant its members liberty and independence.

The troops of the religion ran rampant after the departure of the Japanese and committed many murders and pillaged villages.

The Viet-Minh were also becoming active and collaborated with the Hoa Hao to fight against the French. The Hoa Hao were centralized in the western part of Vietnam. This peaceful co-existence did not last long and the Hoa Hao split from the Viet-Minh and began to fight both sides, the Viet-Minh and the French.

In April of 1947, the Viet-Minh succeeded in killing Huynh Phu So, the founder and leader of the religious sect. This inflamed the people of the sect and they joined forces with the French to fight the communists. Despite this alliance, the Hoa Hao army still lacked discipline and continued to terrorize the countryside and commit numerous crimes. Disagreements caused the army to split three ways. One group fled to the mountains, another to the jungle, and the third collaborated with the Cao Dai religious sect.

The combined group of Cao Dai and Hoa Hao fought with the French while the other two split factions of Hoa Hao fought both sides and terrorized the countryside.

After the defeat of the French and the establishment of the new government in South Vietnam, the Hoa Hao's were still dissident. They, along with the Cao Dai, were brought to defeat by the Republic of Vietnam military forces. The main leader at the time, Ba Cut, was beheaded for his crimes against his fellow Vietnamese by the South Vietnamese government.

The Hoa Hao has never found a successor with the leadership qualities of Huynh Phu So. Whereas in the past it had over a million followers, it is no longer very strong.

The spiritual leadership of the sect is now carried out by the ailing, elderly mother of Huynh Phu So in An Giang province. The government has attempted to reconcile the group, as well as the Cao Dai, in order to gain their support for the government.

TAOISM

Origin Like Confucianism and Buddhism, Taoism came to Vietnam from China centuries ago. There is very limited historical information available about the religion, but traditional stories handed down through generations indicate that it was founded by Lao Tse in China 604 years before the birth of Christ.

Growth Taoism was popular during the early Christian era, but does not appear to have a large religious following in Vietnam today. Instead, the Vietnamese look upon the priests as skilled magicians and diviners. They believe that the priests can help control the spirit world by contact with the Taoist gods. Priests for this religion follow a family line. The father who is a priest teaches his work to his son. Persons of other religions may go to a Taoist priest in cases where they deem magic to be necessary to help them solve their problems.

Beliefs Taoist philosophy centers on the idea of human being's oneness with the universe. They believe that the laws of the universe and nature cannot be changed, one should not try to change them but be content to live with them as best he can under the circumstances. This theory is popular with the Vietnamese and they often stoically accept their lot in life as if there is nothing that they can do about it.

Because of some people's belief that they are powerless against the forces of the universe and man's place in life, they often consider themselves helpless. They then call on the Taoist priests to help them contact the spirits and delay the defeats of death and disaster. Taoists believe in spirits, including demons, ghosts, and the like.

Yogi, a mental physical discipline, is considered to be a part of Taoism. This is a way to accommodate one's self to the surroundings with minimum effort and discomfort.

Magic and sorcery dominate this religion today in Vietnam, and there seems to be little connection with the original religion as founded in China.

OTHER RELIGIOUS GROUPS

In additon to the larger religious sects described in this chapter, many small groups spring up from time to time. A good example of this is the case of the Palm Tree Prophet, a man who has a small following.

Nguyen Thanh Nam is the leader of the Palm Tree Prophets. He spends every evening atop palm trees and towers praying to Buddha and Jesus Christ. In March of 1964, Nam and some of his followers tried to pay a call on American Ambassador Henry Cabot Lodge and Secretary of Defense McNamara right in the middle of an important meeting they were holding at the U.S. Embassy.

He wanted to show the Americans a cat that he had that was nursing several mice. This, he said, proved that people who hate each other can co-exist.

Calling himself a prophet, Nam said he had not bathed in fourteen years. He is well-known in the Delta area of South Vietnam but does not have a large religious following. Many peasants go to him for advice, however.

The Palm Tree Prophet told correspondents gathered at the Embassy that day in March of 1964 that he had the plans that would stop the war in Vietnam. He wanted to travel and see the leaders of the United States, Great Britain, France, Russia, France, Red China, and North Vietnam, in order to ask them to hold an international conference to end the war in Vietnam. The Vietnamese government did not approve his request.

Periodically, the Palm Tree Prophet shows up on the Saigon political scene. Each time there is a new group of leaders, he tries to see them to plead his case. The leaders often say that he is a man being used by the Viet-Cong.

Spiritism Apart from the many religions practiced in Vietnam, many of the people, believe in spirits. There are all kinds of spirits, present between birth and death, and perhaps even before and after these two events. There are good spirits and bad ones, funny ones and stupid ones. There are spirits of people, rocks, animals, trees, of the heavens, kitchen spirits, hearth spirits, master spirits, and subordinate ones. One could go on and on with the list of spirits and what they can supposedly do.

Vietnamese people deal with spirits as the need arises. They have all kinds of ceremonies in which spirits are appeased, scared, tricked, flattered, paid-off, fed, or whatever is called for in the particular case. An example of this may be found in Chapter 10. Appeasing the spirits is most important at Tet, the lunar New Year.

Each small village has its own guardian spirit, and he is worshipped by the whole village in annual ceremonies. Many times, shrines, temples, and buildings called "dinhs" are built for the worship of spirits. Dinhs usually have a high pointed roof. Each occupation such as various handicrafts, fishing, etc. has a guardian spirit.

Many Vietnamese customs, such as not touching another person's head or shoulder, stem from the belief that spirits reside there.

Diviners specialize in spirits and are often called in to "diagnose" which one is causing difficulty and what ceremonies are necessary to appease the spirit.

Spiritism is prevalent in all parts of Vietnam, but is especially strong in the mountain areas with the tribespeople.

Pseudo-Sciences and Fortune Telling Vietnamese rely to a great extent on the advice of pseudo-scientists and fortune tellers when there is an important decision to be made. The pseudo-scientists include astrologers, chiromancers, physiognomists, zoochiromancers, and geomancers.

Astrologers predict the Vietnamese person's future by working with the birth date, including the year, month, day, hour, minute, and where the heavenly bodies were at that time. This is especially important to the Vietnamese when thinking about getting married. Certain times have to be picked by the astrologer as being favorable for events to take place. In addition, the two people's birthdates must be considered harmonious. (See Chapter 6.)

Chiromancers also predict the future, but they do it by reading the palm, to include the lines on the hands and fingers.

Physiognomists foretell the future by studying the shape of the person's head, including the features and brow.

Zoochiromancers carefully inspect boiled rooster feet, especially the joints of the three longer toes. In this manner, they tell the future of the rooster's owner.

A geomancer is called upon when buildings are being erected, for he knows just where they should be situated due to his knowledge of how invisible streams of force flow around the earth creating magnetic fields. Buildings should be placed to agree with these influences. On occasion, if a building is not properly placed for one reason or another, scary looking stone dogs are placed in front of the building to scare away evil spirits.

In addition to these specialists, there are numerous fortune tellers in Vietnam. Many of them can amaze you with their accuracy. They are often poor people who claim that they have seen a vision. They are not usually poor very long after seeing the vision, as people come to them from near and far for advice and to have their fortunes told.

CHRISTIAN RELIGIONS

Catholicism Portuguese and Italian Jesuit missionaries introduced the Catholic religion to Vietnam in the latter part of the 16th century. During the 17th century, Alexander de Rhodes developed " Quoc Ngu," a written, romanized version of spoken Vietnamese. This enabled the Catholics to spread knowledge about their religion and, in addition, was a great help to Vietnamese in many other fields.

In 1658, a Vicar Apostolic was appointed by the Pope in

Rome, and he also made the Catholic church in Vietnam an extension of the Church of France.

During the French period in Vietnam, more converts were made. It is estimated that approximately ten per cent of the population in South Vietnam is Catholic. Many of them are peasants living in the Mekong delta. A large number of Catholics fled the North when the country was divided to escape religious persecution under the communists.

The Catholics have many medical facilities operating in the country, including hospitals, clinics, leprosariums, etc.

The Catholic church of Vietnam is now independent from its connections with the French church. There are quite a few seminaries in the country.

Vietnam has the second largest Catholic population in Asia, after the Philippines.

Protestantism American Protestant missionaries began going to Vietnam at the end of the First World War. Their influence has been limited until recently when it has been greatly expanded. It is estimated that there are over 100,000 Protestants in the country.

The American Christian and Missionary Alliance is the main Protestant activity in Vietnam today. Their activities were centered mostly with the mountain people but is now spreading to other parts of the country. Three of their missionaries, including a woman doctor, have been captured by the Viet-Cong.

The Seven-Day Adventists have a mission in Saigon, including a most popular hospital.

Also in the country are Mennonites. One of their main activities is a medical clinic at Banmethuot.

There is a Baptist church in Saigon on Cach-Mang street.

The Wycliffe Bible translators from California are working on a Vietnamese translation of the Bible, as well as forming written languages, and translating the Bible for the many different mountain tribes.

CHAPTER

5

EDUCATION AND COMMUNICATIONS

Students Students seem extremely serious about their education in Vietnam. As in the past, they bring honor to their families with their success. Many cultures have exerted influence on the student in Vietnam, and methods have changed slowly. Though many Americans think our system is better, much can be learned from the earnestness of the Vietnamese student.

Through the help of the United States, the number of children in school throughout South Vietnam has been raised from 500,000 to one and one-half million in recent years.

This has occurred despite the influence of the Viet-Cong, who try to disrupt the education system and install their own. Even though the Viet-Cong have terrorized students in the past, the little scholars go on. An example of this is evident in that the Viet-Cong will often stop a bus load of children and tell them that if they see them on the bus going to school again, they will cut off one of their hands or make them deaf. After a few days, the students will usually go back to school. The Viet-Cong have frequently made their promise good by stopping the bus again, hacking off hands, or ramming a piece of bamboo into their ears to rupture the eardrums.

Early History of Education in Vietnam

The earliest students in Vietnam received most of their education from the Buddhist clergy. However, with the Chinese domination of the country, Vietnam absorbed much of their educational system. This is especially shown in the early competitive examinations which were held to recruit high mandarinal officials. The first known examination of this type was held in 1075. With the beginning of these examinations, Confucian education replaced that formerly given by the Buddhist clergy.

During the latter part of the 11th century, a National College was established for the education of sons of royalty and other high officials. This marked the beginning of Confucian education in Vietnam. In 1252, the college was opened to students from varied backgrounds other than royal or official.

By the beginning of the 15th century, many Confucian type schools were in operation in leading centers, and education became the most cherished of ideals. Only those who passed the qualifying examinations for Mandarins had any hope of achieving state jobs or other honors. The scholar was looked up to and highly revered.

The Mandarins

All levels of administration in Vietnam were run by Mandarins, who were chosen on the basis of their education alone, up until the time the French ruled in Vietnam.

Technically, any person, no matter wnat his background, could study and take the competitive examinations and, if successful, could become a mandarin. In other words, it was supposed to be a very democratic system of selection enabling the true scholars, regardless of family position, to be promoted into administrative positions.

In actual practice, however, this theory did not hold up as there was interference in the examination process. Numerous references were required from local officials before a person could take the examinations. Persons who were engaged in menial labor, to include shoemakers, actors, etc., plus criminals were excluded from eligibility. In addition, their descendents for three generations were also prohibited from taking the examinations.

There were two branches of the Mandarinate. They were civil (literary) and military, each consisting of nine grades. The top three grades of each merged, and a single Mandarin could hold both titles. Traditionally, mandarins in the literary branch were afforded more prestige than those in the military branch. The literary examinations were different from the military ones; one gave more importance to intellectual qualities while the other tested physical aptitude. This trend was reversed to some extent during the reigns of Gia-Long and Minh-Mang who favored the military side.

How Vietnamese Men became Mandarins

In order to become mandarins, the Vietnamese men had to pass special examinations. In the literary field, there were four large-scale examinations to be taken to reach the top of the Mandarinate. They were the provincial examinations, regional examinations, national competitive examinations, and the court examination.

Provincial Examinations

Before taking the provincial examination, it was necessary for a student to pass four lower level literary tests administered by state-employed professors in the different districts. They chose those students that they thought might be successful in competing in the provincial competitions.

The provincial examinations took place twice yearly. Thousands of students would travel to open-air camps set up for the examinations. The army guarded the camps to prevent any outside help for students taking the exam. Each candidate set up a tent where he carried on his daily routine of sleeping, eating, and working.

Four test sessions, each lasting 24 hours, were given at three to four-day intervals. Each test started at three a.m. when the student was given special paper and sent back to his tent where he wrote until the following midnight.

Excellent ability in the fields of interpretation, verse, composition, and philosophy were essential to the success of the candidate. Scholarships were awarded for further schooling for those doing well on the examinations. The students who excelled above the others were granted one-year exemptions from the armed forces and corvee (forced labor). Those with grades of "good" were exempted for six months. This sometimes caused problems for the local officials in meeting quotas for the armed forces and corvee. To alleviate this problem, the governor of a province often limited the number of competitors from his province by creating more difficult preliminary tests.

Regional Examinations

These were normally held every three years. There was pre-screening of applicants for this examination with additional tests and numerous references required as to character, etc. before admission as a candidate.

Four tests were also administered in the regional examinations; however, these were much harder and longer than at the provincial level. Students passing three of the tests received the title of "Tu Tai" (bachelor) while those passing all four were designated "Cu Nhan" (licentiates). All other candidates failed, and those not passing at least two of the exams were the cause of reprimand to those who recommended them from the provinces.

The examinations were most competitive. An extreme example of this is that during the 19th century, there were usually 12,000 or more candidates in the country at each exam. Of these, only twelve to fifteen licentiate degrees and between 250–500 bachelor degrees were awarded.

Those receiving the lower bachelor degree were excused from military service and the corvee. They could compete in the next regional exams for the higher award, but if they did poorly, they would lose their bachelor's degree. Candidates receiving the license were eligible for appointment as director of studies in a province or district and were allowed to take the national competitive examination for the doctoral degree.

The National Competitive Examination

Those holding the license were allowed to take this

examination which was normally held at three-year intervals. In addition, exceptions were made for those persons from royalty or nobility who held only the bachelor's degree if they had taken special qualifying examinations.

The emperor made up the questions for the examination and those students scoring the highest were eligible to take the court examination. Those scoring in the second group were eligible to re-take the examination and were registered with the Ministry of Personnel and Interior for employment either as a prefect or assistant prefect.

Court Examination

By this time, the number of candidates had been drastically reduced. The emperor personally conducted this examination, and only three of the highest ranking scholars were proclaimed doctors first class. The remainder of the candidates were awarded doctor's degrees in lower classes. The three persons in the first class were entitled to appointments as provincial judicial officers. The others could secure positions in a ministry or prefecture.

French Influence on Education

Before the French came, Mandarins administered Vietnam for approximately 2,000 years. The old-type Mandarin system practically dissolved as the French took over the government's administration and converted it from a Confucian system to a Western-oriented one. Some Mandarins of the old society committed suicide; others rebelled or went into hiding. There were, according to some historical authorities, actual cases in which household servants became Mandarins in the French service and others bought their way in causing great dissatisfaction to the older Mandarins of the Confucian school. This is probably representative only of isolated cases.

In order to participate in the civil service under the French rule, the Vietnamese had to convert to the French system and were required to know the French language. In addition, they had to have a good facility with the new romanized version of their language instead of the traditional Chinese characters which had been in use for hundreds of years.

The French gradually improved their own system of awarding Mandarin degrees and sent many of the Vietnamese officials to France to study Western methods. Reforms were initiated doing away with much of the ritual formerly required by the emperors; retirement provisions and other more modern personnel practices were established; and the new Mandarin class was urged to use more initiative in their work.

Under the old traditional systems, education at the primary level was left to the discretion of communes and private families. Opportunity for higher education, as evidenced in the four examinations heretofore described, was awarded to those who could handle literary forms and styles, rather than just information. The written language was Chinese and the spoken language was Vietnamese. The old educational system placed emphasis on tradition, intellectual pursuits, and moral order.

The French allowed this to co-exist with their system for a while. After the beginning of 1900, the whole system was revised. An educational system of three levels was established; elementary, primary, and secondary education (au hoc, tieu hoc, and trung hoc). In addition, the use of Quoc Ngu, the romanized translation of the spoken language, was added to the curriculum. Emphasis was placed on rote memory, class discipline and other French educational methods.

Many new schools and colleges were established and French became the second language of importance to the students. A new school of Mandarins was established in Hanoi in 1912 with a complete overhaul of the former requirements. New emphasis was placed on the French systems. Graduates were appointed to lower administrative posts not held by French officials.

Vietnamese citizens living in the country were not always afforded the educational benefits of those living in the cities.

Schooling in Recent Years

The school systems have retained most of their French forms in Vietnam. Though the Confucian system is not very important anymore, and men no longer devote their entire lives to learning, the people still have inherited a strong desire for education and deem it very important.

In 1955, a new school system was established after the separation of the country into two parts. The north retained much of the French system with an emphasis on Marxism. The south also retained much of the French system, with an emphasis on nationalism. Vietnamese language, history, and literature are required studies in elementary and secondary schools in the south.

Whereas Vietnamese schools have undergone the influence of the Chinese and the French, they are now influenced by the Americans. A little bit has been salvaged from each culture, however.

The law in South Vietnam provides for free compulsory

education for children over five years of age for the first three grades of primary school. Most of the pupils do not go beyond this compulsory three years. If he goes on, he will take an examination in his fifth year which, if passed, entitles him to a primary certificate.

The secondary school has a seven-year curriculum. In this school, there are two parts, four years and three more. At the end of four years, the student takes an exam. If he passes, he receives a secondary certificate. Few students go beyond this.

At this time, he can go to a vocational school or continue for the second cycle in which he has a choice of continuing the study of modern languages and Vietnamese classics or of taking up natural science, mathematics, or philosophy. Before this time, their education has been more general, much as in the American system.

After the second year of the senior cycle (sixth year of secondary school), another examination must be passed. The successful student receives the Baccalaureate I. At the completion of the third year of the senior cycle (seventh year), he may compete for the Baccalaureate II, which is necessary to enter the university system or advanced technical schools.

In addition to these public institutions, there are numerous private schools which have sprung up offering courses in English. It is not uncommon to see Vietnamese of all ages enrolled in one of these extra-curricula schools. Numerous Americans have taught in these schools in their off-duty time.

There are also private schools run by religious and organizational groups. Some are French. These have been closely administered in the past and must comply with the South

Vietnamese government standards. At the Chinese Free Pacific Institute in Cholon, for example, the Vietnamese language is taught, women instructors must not wear the Chinese dress, and the principal must be of Vietnamese citizenship. This has been relaxed somewhat since the coup d'etat of 1963.

Adult education is encouraged. Where possible, classes are held for adults in the provinces in the evenings in an attempt to raise the literacy rate which hovers around 30 per cent.

The Vietnamese-American Association has expanded considerably during its brief history in Vietnam. There are normally about 7,000 students enrolled in language courses and vocational fields. This association has begun to extend its activities into other cities in Vietnam besides Saigon. In the past, teachers have been mostly Americans, drawn from the official agency employees in their off-duty time and from families of Americans living in Vietnam. When the majority of American dependents were evacuated from Vietnam in February of 1965, an acute shortage of teachers resulted for the various English language schools, including the Vietnamese-American Association.

The desire to learn English is quite strong among the Vietnamese and is a good example of the Vietnamese and their strong desire to keep up with the changing times in their country.

University Training

Students possessing the Baccalaureate II and passing entrance examinations are entitled to enter a university in Vietnam. There are three available, Saigon University, University of Dalat, and Hue University.

The University of Saigon is the largest with a reported 17,000 students enrolled in 1965. A break-down of student enrollment showed: Law School 4,348; Science 3,966; Letters 3,496; Pharmacy 2,107; Medicine 1,294; Pedagogy 826; and Architecture 465. The figures may be slightly high, as it is not too uncommon to find one student registered and taking courses in more than one school, and there is little cross-checking between the faculties.

Each faculty is separate from the other and acts independently. Therefore, the education offered has been narrowly specialized with little benefit to general education. There is no such thing as required courses for all students in broad fields of science, mathematics, languages, etc. as we find in American colleges and universities.

Attendance in classes, for the most part, is not demanded. A student may study independently or obtain notes from other students and pass the examinations. Little outside reading is demanded and a student can take the professor's notes, study the text and reasonably expect to pass. The student expects the teachers to be "all-knowing" and generally does not understand the directed research system which is popular in American universities, especially at the graduate level.

Examinations assume great importance in the Vietnamese educational system, with those coming at the end of the term determining whether students go on to the next course of instruction.

Overseas Training

Large numbers of students leave Vietnam for further study. The French sent students to their country during their rule in Vietnam, and many students continue to go there to further their education today. Now, the trend is for students to go to the United States. In addition to the hundreds of Vietnamese military men who have been trained in certain fields in the United States, numerous civilians have gone to the United States to study courses which are not available to them in their own country. Many families will suffer great sacrifices to send one of their children abroad. Often, in the past, students have been allowed to leave the country to study only at the whim of the government in power. This has been a deciding factor in just who is allowed to go, and perhaps some of the most deserving students have been denied this privilege. In the past, it was not unusual for a student's family to pay large sums of money to facilitate getting a passport. I do not know the circumstances of this situation today, but hope that improvement has been made.

Communication Media Communications in Vietnam can be both frustrating and fascinating. Prior to the arrival of the Americans, communications in the field of telephones and radio communication was very limited. American military programs including men and aid have helped to alleviate some of the main problems, but they are far from being completely solved.

TELEPHONES

One must maintain a good sense of humor when using the telephone in Vietnam. There are very few people who have telephones in their homes, because of inadequate lines and switching equipment, and the cost of telephone service is prohibitive. Americans in Vietnam find it hard to operate without telephones and have installed large numbers.

Getting into the military switchboard from a civilian number requires patience, fortitude, and an even temper. The American switch in Saigon is named "Tiger." When on a military line and trying to call a civilian number, one must also go through Tiger. The lines seem to be forever busy, and you may well get someone who tells you, "no, this is not tiger, this is pussycat," which is just his way of letting you know that you have the wrong number. Other American switchboards in the country have animal names. They are hard to reach but are a vast improvement over the past when no systems were available at all.

The Vietnamese use their servants or messengers to take messages for them. As for those with telephones, the Bell System would shriek in horror at the telephone manners.

It is possible to call abroad from Vietnam. Calls have to be made at a certain time of day for different countries. Often, weather interferes with communications. It is best to make a reservation in advance to make a call. In addition to those calling at the PTT (government-owned post, telephone, and telegraph), long lines of Americans wait each morning at the radio station in Saigon where they often get better connections and service.

Telegraph Service

Available in South Vietnam's major cities and for service abroad.

Newspapers

The Vietnamese must love to read newspapers because there are more papers published in Saigon for the number of people in the city, than any other city in the world. A few of these are distributed outside of the city.

Often, the coverage borders on the sensational side. Consequently, newspapers are often closed by the government. The people want a free press, but unfortunately, they do not have enough experience with freedom of the press to understand that responsibility is also required of journalists. This, of course, does not apply to all of the professional journalists, but mainly refers to those "fly by night" editors who frequently bring out new and sensational publications.

In some cases, the papers have been closed by the government for criticism of the government's practices and policies. On the other hand, some of the presses closed have been infiltrated by the communists.

The Vietnamese like to read serial love stories, and poems, and no self-respecting newspaper could survive without ghost stories and horoscopes.

Two English language newspapers in South Vietnam are the *Saigon Daily News* and the *Saigon Post.*

Radio

There was no television in Vietnam until February 7, 1966 when the Americans commenced operations of two channels; one in the Vietnamese language, and the other in English. Still, most of the Vietnamese people are served by radio. They like to hear sentimental music and love stories. Many of the broadcasters are women. The government operates the main stations. Reception is also clear from other nearby countries including the Philippines and North Vietnam. The Voice of America and Radio Hanoi both come in loud and clear.

There is an American station, Armed Forces Radio, in South Vietnam today. It is also popular with the Vietnamese who are studying English and those who like to listen to the latest music from America. The French have also had a station in Vietnam.

Radio Catinat When someone hears the term, "Radio Catinat," they may think it is a special radio station. In reality, it is a gossip grape-vine which entwines the city of Saigon. It seems to be pin-pointed at Tu-Do Street, which was formerly called Catinat, and this is the reason for its name.

The street seems to be a home for those who stop and say to each other, "You tell me your rumor and I'll tell you mine." Radio Catinat is often amazingly accurate as to what is happening in the government and other official circles. There seems to be nothing like Radio Catinat in the U.S.

Tu-Do is an interesting street in the heart of Saigon where people of different backgrounds and nationalities congregate in various sections. For instance, American journalists often meet at the Hotel Caravelle Bar. Other foreign press appear to like Brodards, a delightful air-conditioned restaurant, coffee-house, and ice-cream bar combined, further down the street. The French seem to prefer the Imperial Hotel. American GI's congregate at the bars on Tu-Do, and women of all nationalities frequent the fancy shops. Indians have stores all along this street.

CHAPTER 6

CUSTOMS AND RITES

ANYONE going to Vietnam would be wise to bone up on some of the unique customs and superstitions of the country, lest they cause confusion, misunderstandings, hard-feelings, or loss of friendship. The old saying, "when in Rome, do as the Romans do" cannot be applied to the letter in Vietnam, but it is still very important that we respect certain customs and superstitions of the people.

Many Vietnamese having extensive contact with Americans have begun to understand American ways and have even adopted some of them for their own use. However, there are thousands of ordinary folk whose customs have not changed in generations. This chapter is about those people.

Greeting People

Most of the Vietnamese in urban areas no longer bow when they meet each other. In formal gatherings, at religious places, and sometimes in the country areas, one may see the people clasp their hands together in a prayer-like gesture and bow slightly. This is not practiced to any extent in everyday life in Vietnam as it is in neighboring Thailand.

The custom of handshaking, formerly considered barbaric to the Vietnamese, is now achieving popularity due to the Western influence in the country. Men will generally shake hands and say the equivalent of "how are you" and tip their hats when greeting people. Women, especially those in the countryside, still shy away from shaking hands, especially with men from their own country. It is best not to offer to shake hands with a woman unless she offers her hand first.

Introductions Whereas Americans often immediately introduce themselves in given situations, the ordinary people of Vietnam think this to be rather bold and like to have a mutual acquaintance make the introduction. They will rarely introduce themselves when going into a home or office until asked to do so. This may be due to their innate shyness and modesty.

Names carry great importance in Vietnam. Often Vietnamese will have secret names, known only to themselves and their parents. If it is given away, the person believes he is exposed to evil spirits. Except in rare cases, family names are seldom used outside of the family circle. Children are often called names in rank of birth, such as Chi-hai; Chi-ba (daughter two, daughter three).

One should call Vietnamese people by Mr., Mrs., or Miss until asked to go on a first name basis. They do not do this as quickly as Americans in their relationships with people. Especially important, when in the company of a third person, your friend must be called by his name with a Mr., Miss, or Mrs. preceeding it, as the case may be. If this is not done, it may suggest great intimacy or friendliness, or can also be interpreted as being arrogant treatment of the individual by a superior.

Most Vietnamese names consist of a family name, middle name and a personal or given name. The order is reverse to the American custom. For instance, John Paul Jones' name in Vietnamese style would be Jones Paul John. However, we do not call someone by his family name in Vietnam. If we use the name for instance, Miss Hau Dinh Cam. Hau is the family name. We would call her Miss Cam. Jones Paul John would be Mr. John. On very informal occasions, we might at their request call them Cam or John, but would always add a Miss or Mr. to the name in the presence of other people outside of the group.

An exception to this rule dates back to traditional customs of long ago when beloved leaders were called by their family names.

It is desirable to call Vietnamese professional and government officials by their title, i.e., Mr. Assemblyman, Mr. Doctor, Mr. Lieutenant, etc.

Taboos in Personal Relationships It is best to call to people in a quiet voice, using their names preceded by Mr. Mrs., or Miss. Waving or beckoning with an upturned finger is considered highly impolite. If you must silently signal for someone to come toward you, do so by using the whole hand with the palm turned down. Not to do so would indicate an air of authority or superiority over the person being called or beckoned.

Never touch anyone on the head as this would be considered as a personal insult to the individual and perhaps even to his ancestors. Many Vietnamese believe the spirit resides there. Hence, the belief that if a person is beheaded, his spirit will roam forever without finding a resting place. Also, don't touch anyone on the shoulder. Some people believe that a genie resides there and it is undesirable to disturb him. If you mistakenly touch one shoulder, you must also touch the other shoulder and this helps offset the bad luck.

Confusing Personal Traits of Vietnamese

Vietnamese people have a habit of not looking into your eyes when they talk to you. This is often because of shyness, but one of the main reasons is that traditionally they do not look into the eyes of those they respect or those higher in rank when talking to them. This is to indicate politeness.

The smile of a Vietnamese can be very confusing in Vietnam to an outsider and cause misunderstandings. In some Oriental countries, a smile can mean sorrow, worry, or embarrassment. In Vietnam, it may indicate a polite, but perhaps skeptical reaction to something, compliance or toleration of a blunder or misunderstanding, or on occasion represents submission to a judgment that may be wrong or unfair. This is particularly true if the one making the judgment is at a superior level and perhaps has lost his temper. For instance, a laundress may ruin a favorite shirt and is called in by her employer to be asked about it. She may smile. This does not mean that she thinks it is funny that she burned the shirt, but instead is submission to the fact. If the owner of the shirt loses his temper, she may keep smiling indicating politeness or patience with superiors.

Because of this, foreigners should be very cautious in voicing their opinions and perhaps be a little more delicate, more tolerant and restrain from being obstinate.

Loud arguments or heated discussions are frowned upon and are seldom heard among the Vietnamese. Well-bred people are trained in self-discipline. It is best, therefore, for Americans or other foreigners to do their best to keep tempers in check, no matter what the circumstances, lest they be looked upon with disdain.

Vietnamese seldom use a direct approach in their dealings. To do so indicates a lack of tact or delicacy. Directness is appreciated in the Western world, but not in Vietnam. The Vietnamese do not like to say "no" and will often reply "yes" when the answer should be negative. This problem is further complicated by Americans posing negative questions such as, "It doesn't look like it will rain today, does it?" The correct answer is often the one given by the Vietnamese—"Yes." We expect to hear "No." Think it out and you will see that the Vietnamese is really correct.

Best advice, don't ask negative questions.

Superstitions There are numerous taboos on all aspects of life in Vietnam, just as we have our omens of bad luck such as walking under a ladder. A few of them are as follows:

Don't express lavish admiration for a new baby, because the devils might hear you and steal the child because of his desirability.

When going somewhere on business, avoid seeing a woman first. If you do see a woman first as you go out your door or on the way, postpone the trip.

Mirrors are often placed on front doors. If a dragon tries to get in, he will see his reflection and think that there is already a dragon there and go away.

Single bowls of rice and chopsticks should not be served. Always place at least two on a table. One bowl is for the dead. Never let chopsticks touch others or make unnecessary noise with them. Do not place chopsticks in food and leave them there.

Do not hand someone a toothpick.

Never buy one pillow or mattress pad, always buy two.

Do not use relative's towels.

Do not overturn musical instruments, or beat both sides of a drum simultaneously.

Do not cut finger and toenails at night.

Going dutch with a Vietnamese is not appreciated. If you run into someone at a restaurant and you join his table, let him pay the whole bill or pay it all yourself. The senior person usually pays.

Gifts for brides and grooms are usually given in pairs, including blankets. A single item indicates the marriage is not expected to last long. Two less expensive items are more desired than one nicer one.

Educated people and others who are not in the peasant class do not work with their hands. To do so would appear to try to beat a poor peasant out of his job. In addition, it is considered beneath the dignity of refined people.

Hats are not usually worn inside churches, even Catholic ones.

Hospitality Except among the higher officials, the average wage of a Vietnamese family is below that even conceived of being adequate. The old argument is, "well, things cost less," but this is not completely true in Vietnam. The prices on some items, considered necessities by Americans, such as electricity, are exorbitant. Compared with the average Vietnamese income, clothing and food prices are also high, especially during a time of war. An average family may earn the equivalent of $50 a month with two or more people working in the family.

Despite this, the Vietnamese love to be hospitable and will often invite you to dinner. They may solicit the entire neighborhood borrowing things to make your stay more pleasant, or they may sell something they have had for a long time in order to have the money to entertain you well. They enjoy being good hosts and would feel hurt if you mentioned this to them. It is best to pretend that you know nothing of this. Do not offer to share the costs. When reciprocating, do so in a lavish style at the very best of restaurants.

If gifts are taken for the family, they should be items that they could not easily obtain themselves. To take something that they could buy easily would be a bad reflection on their economic means. They love anything American, and it does not have to be expensive. If you give the children things, each should have a separate gift. It is not polite to take a whole bag of candy and give it to them as a group.

On short visits, drink the tea that is offered, even if you don't like it and are afraid of the local water. It shows that you are welcome and well respected.

Rank is always carefully observed by the Vietnamese in

their homes and elsewhere. Servants never sit at the same table with their employers if outsiders are present, and only in rare cases otherwise.

On some occasions at an informal meal, the whole family except for the person inviting you to dinner, may get up from the table and eat elsewhere. This is not a show of disrespect for you but is simply a way of letting the guest spend time with his special friend.

At banquets, one should arrive on time and greet elderly persons first. If the dinner is served Chinese style, food should be transferred from the main bowl to your individual bowl before eating. It is impolite to eat anything with your chopsticks directly from the serving bowl. A guest may refrain from taking something he doesn't like, but if the hostess serves it to you unknowingly, force it down if at all possible. If the guest refuses, the host may doubt his sincerity and coax him even more. Individual bowls are usually changed with each course and are generally removed only when empty, except the last course. Here, a little something should be left to indicate to the host that there was enough food and everyone is satisfied.

In order not to hurt your host's feelings, it is best to go to one of these parties with a hearty appetite and an open mind along with a good strong stomach. Sometimes foods are served that are repugnant to Americans. On many occasions, an American will be the honored guest and naturally served the most honored piece of chicken—its head. To refuse it is an insult. Some of the more Westernized Vietnamese know of the Americans' disdain for this particular part of the chicken and often give it to them to amuse themselves or to test the Americans' manners. Most often, they are very sincere in offering you the piece most desired by themselves.

MARRIAGE

In Vietnam today, there are two distinct groupings as far as the important rite of marriage is concerned. One group is the more modern, who cling to Western innovations and desire similar weddings. The following section will concern itself with the second group and its traditional rites of engagement and marriage which are highly regarded and practiced in Vietnam.

Pre-Marriage Relationships In olden days, chastity was strongly emphasized with young people being carefully supervised. As with Confucianism, the physical development of love was not highly regarded. Parents frowned on courtship and falling in love and thought badly of its advocates.

Marriage was considered to be a duty, and was generally arranged in a non-emotional manner by the elders in the family. Sometimes, mere children have been committed to each other for later marriage.

Formerly, couples readily submitted to the parents choosing their mates and still do to a great extent in the countryside. In the cities, they have begun to "fight for their rights." Youngsters have more opportunities to meet each other these days, so often the role of the parents has been cut down to merely advising and counseling.

Choice of Marriage Partners Certain standards should be maintained in the choice of mate under the traditional system. For instance, social rank, education, moral history, etc. should be similar in background and on as equal a level as possible.

The couple's horoscope should be in accord and not conflict. Horoscope data has been deliberately misread on occasions in order to be able to tactfully refuse an offer of marriage. Usually a mediator works between the families, and if successful, is often rewarded with a present, such as a pig's head.

Age at Marriage Formerly, girls were often wed as early as 13 and boys at 16. Economic reasons often spurred on young marriages. For example, one family may have wished to have their daughter marry so that they would have one less mouth to feed. On the boy's side, a wife would mean another helping hand in the field, plus the prospect of more children to work on the land.

Daughter-in-laws were considered to be "free domestic help," and many girls were older than their bride-grooms. On occasions, marriages were held for very young couples to bring about alliances between families.

In Vietnam today, the marriage age may range from 16 to 18 for women and 20 to 21 for men. These figures rise to higher age levels in the cities where the Western influence is felt. Child marriages are not so common in Vietnam today.

Rituals Though many things have changed, the rituals have stayed more or less the same in traditional marriages. A description of each of the important rituals follows.

Presenting Gifts This is often called "the crossing of the girl's housegate." It is a time when the boy's family brings the girl's family gifts which must include a bunch of betel leaves and areca nuts. Tea, cakes, and candies may also be included. The day and hour must be exactly right by the horoscopic calendar.

The procedure is usually quite formal with everyone dressed in his best clothing. Led by a distinguished elder member of the boy's family, the family walks to the girl's home. Boys dressed in black with red sashes around their waists carry the gifts on round red trays balanced on their heads. The bridegroom and the intermediary or matchmaker are also present. The matchmaker will discuss the gifts that the bridegroom will later present to the bride's family. The date for the formal proposal of marriage is set at this time.

The wedding gifts that the bride's family request will be given to relatives and friends of the girl's family. The gifts are often sets of tea, candies, areca nuts, betel leaves, etc. These gifts are in addition to the ones brought to the home on this day. If the girl's parents have a wide circle of friends, then a large number of gifts are required.

In addition to these, the bridegroom's family must provide the bride with a trousseau of jewels such as engagement ring, earrings, necklaces, bracelets, and perhaps even a certain amount of money.

Formal Proposal of Marriage The horoscope must be consulted for the right time and hour, and once again the entourage of family and friends descend on the bride's home in much the same manner in the "gift presenting ceremony." At the home of the bride-to-be, they are graciously received with tea, areca nuts, betel leaves, and perhaps liquor being served. The gifts brought by the bridegroom-to-be are placed on the ancestral altar. Joss sticks and lights are lit and incense is burned. The girl's father, the future bride and groom ceremonially bow before the altar. After this, the bride may withdraw to another room and her future husband may take over the entertainment of the guests, acting as a member of the bride's family.

After a long period of conversation, the head of the girl's family removes the gifts from the altar, thanks everyone, and divides the edible gifts into two parts, one smaller than the other. The smaller part is given back to the groom's family indicating that they have been far too generous and that the bride's family is not greedy. This also indicates good luck and a close alliance between the two families. Later, the other edible gifts are distributed to friends of the bride's family.

In the past, the waiting time from this date until the actual marriage was sometimes as long as two or three years. All the while, the bridegroom-to-be was supposed to keep up his relationship with his fiancee's family with generous gifts on many special days. Today, this waiting period has been drastically reduced. The man was not allowed to see the girl very often and then they were closely supervised. Should they by chance meet in public, the bride-to-be would cover her face discreetly with her hat. Instead of being dismayed, this made the future groom proud, as it indicated to all that his future wife was chaste. This old custom has changed considerably in Vietnam today. There are, however, those in the rural areas who still maintain these practices.

The Wedding Celebration

Horoscopes are especially important for the wedding and numerous checks are made, for no one would want to start a marriage off on the wrong foot. Usually the day before the wedding, the boy's family has a banquet. Among the poor, it may be a tea party or nothing at all.

On the wedding day, the family of the bridegroom go with the groom at a specially chosen hour to the bride's home. They all walk together in a procession which is normally led by an old man in dark robes carrying an incense burner. The groom's parents and older relatives follow the elderly man. Next in line is the bridegroom dressed in new clothes and surrounded by his numerous attendants. They are followed by the brothers and sisters and close friends. Women carry betel leaves and areca nuts and offer them to the wedding party en route.

The procession on foot is common in rural areas, especially among the poorer people. It is a status symbol to be able to have other means of transportation in the procession and a great deal of money is often spent by those wishing to make a good impression on others. It is not unusual in large cities to see such processions made up of fancy cars bedecked with garlands of flowers.

When they reach the bride's home, they are welcomed and invited in by the girl's parents. The parents never come out beyond the gate of the home, as they do not wish to appear as initiating the move of offering their daughter's hand in marriage.

After sipping tea, the head of the boy's family makes a solemn formal request to take the bride away to their home where she will be a daughter-in-law to the family. Solemnly, the father or head of the girl's family agrees.

Then the girl's father or head of the family performs a rite in front of the family altar, requesting acceptance of the marriage by his ancestors. The bride and groom follow suit.

A banquet is often held at this point, but near the end, the groom's family traditionally acts as though they are very anxious to take the bride to their home.

The groom's entourage then begins the trip home in procession, with the bride and her attendants, friends and relatives joining in.

Little children sometimes set up road blocks and ask tolls of the wedding party. These are readily paid, as they consider it bad luck to refuse.

Upon arrival at the groom's house, the party is met by the loud noise of firecrackers. The guests are invited inside with the bride and groom and another ceremony which honors the genie of marriage soon commences.

The genie of marriage is often called the Rose Silk Thread God and is believed to be responsible for the couple getting married. A special altar is set up and lighted with candles, and incense and joss sticks are burned in honor of the genie. An older member of the groom's family leads the ceremony. He and the bridal couple bow many times before the altar, and a red sheet of paper on which a plea for aid and protection is written to the genie of marriage. This is read aloud. Three cups are filled with a clear white alcoholic beverage by the elder man leading the ceremony. The old man bows three times and gives one cup to the groom who sips a little of the liquid and passes it to his bride who also sips a little. The groom takes some ginger and rubs it in salt, eats a little of it and then shares it with his bride. This symbolizes that no matter what happens, their love will remain true. The sheet of red paper is then burned and the three people bow once again paying their final respects to the genie.

At this point, the couple are considered married and a party is usually held with a lot of speech making, gift giving and merrymaking.

Just as in the United States, the groom's attendants try to keep him busy as long as they can and play jokes on him. In olden days, the bride and groom spent their first night of marriage in separate rooms with their attendants.

The couple usually live with the husband's parents, at least until children are born. It is expected that the bride will wait on her husband's family, almost as a servant. This is not the custom with the educated and well-to-do class of people in Vietnam. They are somewhat Westernized in their approach.

PREGNANCY AND BIRTH

EXCEPT AMONG young moderns, one of the greatest desires of the Vietnamese is to have a large family. Boys are more desired than girls and are especially important to carry on the family line and ancestral worship. A couple having only girls are looked upon by many as having done something wrong in their lives and are, therefore, being punished.

Traditional customs dictate that the mother-to-be must follow strict rules and observe certain customs and taboos in order to have a good healthy baby. She should eat only nourishing foods, but not so nourishing that they would cause the baby to become too big before birth. The mother must carry on prenatal education with her baby, acting and talking as if he was in her presence at all times, guiding and counseling him in physical, intellectual, and moral activities. Alcohol and cigarettes are considered undesirable for the expectant mother.

Pregnant women are often discouraged from undertaking heavy work and getting involved in tense situations. In some lower economic strata, this is impossible, but still desirable.

An expectant mother should not go to weddings and funerals as it is believed that her presence could bring bad luck to the families concerned. It is also considered bad luck for a pregnant woman to meet people about to set out on a trip. Mothers-to-be should not step over a hammock lest their child be born lazy. They should not walk too much, reach for things high up, take long uncomfortable rides or frequent places of worship.

Midwives generally deliver babies and cut the umbilical cord with a piece of earthenware or a bamboo knife. The baby is then washed and dressed in old handed-down clothes of his brothers and sisters. Vietnamese people fear that the evil spirits will be jealous of new clothes and cause the baby to become ill. The father may see the child only after the baby has been cleaned and dressed.

Friends send the mother nourishing food, and the baby gold bracelets, clothing and trinkets. The baby's hair and nails must never be cut during the first month of life.

Wherever possible, the mother is encouraged not to do any strenuous work for at least two to three months. Among the peasantry, they are often back at work within a few days, because of necessity.

Celebrations After approximately one-month, the newborn baby's parents have a large party to celebrate the baby's first month birthday. Offerings are presented at this time to the "Holy Godmother" who is thought to be the protector of the new child. They also believe that the Holy Godmother teaches the baby to smile and that crying means the child is being punished for stubborness. During the ceremony, a flower which has been wet with special water from the altar is held over the baby and the water is allowed to drip into the infant's mouth. This is to insure that the child will learn to speak in sweet scented words.

After the prayers and ceremonies, guests have a happy party at which they eat the offerings of food from the ceremony. At this time, it is considered correct to put new clothes on the baby, but care is still observed in not mentioning the good health of the child lest the evil spirits become jealous and make him ill.

The baby has another celebration after one lunar year. It is called "quitting the cradle." This is a much larger party with numerous guests. The baby is placed on a bed in a sitting position. Several things are spread around him including scissors, flowers, books, pencils, etc. The item the baby picks up first is supposed to determine his future avocation. If he takes the scissors, he may become a tailor; the book, a learned man, etc.

A baby is considered to be one year of age at birth and becomes two years old when the next lunar New Year arrives. It is possible, therefore, for a child to become two years old when he is just one day old if he is born on New Year's Eve.

FUNERALS

VIETNAMESE spend far more of their income on funerals than Americans do. This may seem impossible in view of the high costs in the United States, but it is true. A family may use all of its worldly goods that can be transferred into money or they may borrow from various association. If this is not possible, they may go into great debt with "money sharks" to pay for funerals.

Catholic funerals follow the ritual of that church, but most funerals are Buddhist since a majority of the population follow that or related religions.

Death The Vietnamese strongly believe that a person should die at home and be surrounded by his family. It is considered to be a bad misfortune to die away from home and bad luck to carry a corpse home. Many people are carried to the hospital if they are sick, but if it becomes evident that they will die, they are rushed home with all possible haste so that their demise may be made there.

The face of the dead person is covered with a white piece of paper or a kerchief as a symbolic barrier between the dead person and the living one. This also helps to shield visitors from too great an emotional shock.

Often, the deceased person's mouth is propped open so that visitors may drop in grains of rice and gold coins. The body is generally placed on a bed under a mosquito net. In some areas, a bunch of bananas are placed on the stomach of the dead person with the hope of distracting the devil from devouring the dead person's intestines. Sometimes a knife is placed on the stomach as a weapon against the devil.

Family members wash the body with a heavily scented lotion and dress it in the best clothing. Nails are cut and the trimmings are placed in small packages and attached to the proper hand and foot from which they were cut. Three years later, when the body is exhumed and the bone transferred from the wooden coffin to an earthenware box for final burial, these clippings will help the people identify the correct bones.

Meanwhile, among the more well-to-do, an obituary has been placed in the paper and friends begin to descend on the home. Among the poor people, the sad news is transmitted by word of mouth.

In the past, caskets were often bought ahead of time, and in mountain areas, the coffin is used in the house as a bench. In towns and cities, this practice has been abandoned.

During olden days, the body was kept in the home for as long as six months, sealed inside the casket. Currently, the body is kept at home about a week or less.

Sometimes, coffins are temporarily buried in the gardens to discourage thieves from robbing the valuables inside. In the case of young virgin girls, the burial place is often nearby the home so that it can be watched. Some rural people believe that the head of a virgin girl is very valuable and may be conserved and turned into the most powerful and omnipotent talisman through special ceremonies. Persons who have the talisman are believed to be omnipotent and invulnerable.

Before the body is placed in the coffin, it is wrapped with strips of cloth and a white silk shroud. The body is wedged in the coffin with reed branches, paper, and other objects. This helps keep the body in place as it decomposes. Embalming is not widely practiced. A bowl of uncooked rice is placed on the lid of a coffin by many families. They believe that this will keep the dead body from arising. The coffin should be attended constantly to keep any dog or cat from jumping over it, as it is believed that if this happens, the body will be revived temporarily and behave erratically, scaring those present.

The family then gather before the special altar which has been erected for the dead person, and make offerings of food for the dead person's soul. This usually is three bowls of rice, three cups of tea, and a few other special dishes. In North Vietnam, it may be different—one bowl of rice, one cup of water, a boiled egg, and a bundle of joss sticks planted in a bowl of uncooked rice and surrounded by lightened candles. This ceremony is supposed to be repeated three times a day during the entire mourning period, but in recent years, the time of this offering has been reduced to an acceptable 100 days.

Dressing in mourning clothes is also a ritual. If there is a wedding planned in the family, it should be quietly attended to before the ceremony of handing out the mourning clothes. Otherwise, custom dictates that the wedding must be postponed until the end of the mourning period.

The mourning period is three years for wives, children, daughter-in-laws, and adopted children of the deceased man and only one year by husband's, son-in-laws, brothers, sistters, nephews, nieces, and grandchildren of a woman. Nine months is the time of mourning for cousins on the father's side, and five months by cousins on the mother's side.

While in mourning, Vietnamese do not usually visit temples and pagodas, festivals, parties, and other entertainments.

They also normally delay marriages and do not wear bright colored clothing. A black band is worn on the arm by men in mourning and a small black piece of material is worn on the dress of women mourners after the funeral for the entire mourning period.

Funeral Dress The ceremony of distribution of the mourning garb is carried out by monks or the eldest son of the deceased who leads the rite. Offerings are made and symbolic votive papers are burned. The mourning garb is made of a very low grade white gauze and looks as if it may fall off of the person wearing it. Turbans are carelessly wrapped around the head with straw crowns and a sash placed on top of this. Mourners use walking sticks made of bamboo and act as though they are groping their way along and would fall without the stick's support. The carelessness of dress and the groping walk are indications of how overcome the mourners are.

Only after the distribution of mourning garb do the presentations of condolences begin. At this time, friends may bring or send gifts to the deceased's family as an offering to the dead member. Sometimes in rural areas, this gift consists of money.

Wreaths have begun to be popular in the cities. They write the name of the person sending them in large letters, and a sympathy message is written on a ribbon encircling the wreath.

The Funeral Procession One of the main expenses of the funeral comes at this point. Many special funeral accoutrements are needed. They may sometimes be borrowed from a community benevolent association, in the case of poor people. Musicians must be hired, numerous attendants are necessary and a huge ten-foot high hearse painted with many dragons and other figures is used. A family will occasionally hire extra mourners to walk in the procession to indicate that the deceased was well thought of. Huge displays of expensive food including whole pigs and gelatined fruits, etc. are placed on tables and carried by bearers.

Buddhist monks, sometimes carried in a hammock, lead the procession. He is usually followed by a group of old ladies carrying long pieces of cloth above their heads. Banner carriers move alongside of them reciting prayers and holding up their banners written about the deceased, for all to read. Next comes the altar, also borne by carriers. On it will be placed a picture of the deceased, two peanut oil lamps, candlesticks, incense burners, and flowers.

Next comes the offerings of food; roasted pig, sugar cakes, rice, gelatined fruits, wine in urns, etc.

Following that is the hearse which is pulled by four to eight persons. In olden days, the coffin was often covered by expensive votive papers in the form of a house. Some of the hearses are motorized in the cities.

After the hearse, the family, led by the eldest son, relatives, and friends follow behind, usually walking. The family is always crying loudly and lamenting in loud tearful voices their praise of the dead person, his virtues, and his accomplishments. Sometimes they cry over what they might have done for the deceased. Their voices, mixed in with the music from the professional musicians playing wind and string instruments and trumpets produce a soulful sound. To Western ears, it sounds more like screeching. The music is chosen especially for the deceased as they have different songs to fit different circumstances.

Acquaintances walk behind this group, remaining fairly silent, exchanging a few words here and there about the life of the dead person. Friends born in the same year as the deceased rarely attend the funeral lest they also have very bad luck or even die. In the case of a wealthy person or a well-known one, large numbers of cyclos carrying flowers trail after these mourners. Along the route, golden votive papers are scattered as symbolic money for the dead person to use in heaven.

When the body reaches its resting place and is about to be placed in the grave, the wailing and crying grows even more soulful, and close relatives often fight frenziedly with the bearers of the coffin to prevent them from burying their loved one.

The eldest son, the monk, or funeral attendants throw a symbolic handful of dirt into the grave and then pass on their respects to the rest of the family. Relatives leave the grave but wait a short distance away until the grave is completely covered before they go home.

In rural areas, the custom of preparing a large meal for all friends and acquaintances who have participated in the funeral or sent a gift is still followed.

Later, a special altar that had been previously set up for the dead member is lighted with candles continuously and incense sticks burned for 100 days.

Regular ceremonies are held for the dead person after that

time, especially on the death anniversary, the lunar New Year period (Tet) and often on the 1st and 15th days of each lunar month.

Families normally have a special dinner on the 49th and 100th day after the death and also on the first anniversary. They may have a dinner every year after that on the death anniversary.

When the body is exhumed three years later and the bones are cleaned and re-arranged in proper order and reburied in a small earthenware coffin, only relatives and close friends are in attendance, and no special social gathering is held.

The veneration of the dead person with special offerings of food and votive papers in the form of money, clothing, etc. continues throughout the years. For more information, see Chapters 4 and 10.

CHAPTER

7

ARTS

ART FORMS in Vietnam have been influenced by outsiders for years to include the Chinese, the French, and the Americans. In spite of these influences, the Vietnamese have emerged in many ways as their own masters.

Architecture There is nothing too unusual about Vietnamese architecture today. It appears to be a melting pot made up of buildings constructed with available materials, such as wood, bamboo, and thatch. Concrete is now being used for big buildings in the large cities and towns. The design used is similar to those found in China, France, and the United States.

In the larger cities, such as Saigon, Hue, and Dalat, some buildings look very much like those found in France. These are typified by thick stone walls and high ceilings. Today, the influence of the Americans is being felt in the newer and more modern buildings which are typical of modern architecture adapted to a tropical climate. This is particularly true of schools being built in South Vietnam.

The influence of the Chinese is seen in the temples, pagodas, tombs, and burial places. At these sites, one finds pillared porches bedecked by dragons and other traditional motifs. Wide expanses of roof with decorated supporting beams are dominant.

The most common housing, found in the countless villages in Vietnam, both north and south, is made up of single-storied buildings made with sun-baked walls, no floor at all, thatched roofs, etc. Woven mats are placed on the floor and beaded blinds shield the doors and divide the rooms.

Due to wars, the effects of time, termites and lack of durability of materials, little is left of the famous architecture of the past including the palaces of Co-Loa, Hoa-Lu, and Thang-Long. Of the ones left standing, though in ruins, a little insight can be gained into Vietnamese architecture of the past. Some of these include the One Column Pagoda in North Vietnam, the Temple of Confucius (1700) at Hanoi, pagodas at Phat-Tieh, and the Palaces and Imperial grounds in Hue. Also still standing are remnants of the Chams and their long stay in Vietnam.

Sculpture Architecture and sculpture go hand in hand in Vietnam; once the Vietnamese buildings were in place, the sculptor went to work decorating columns, pillars, beams, and panels.

Foreign influence is also felt in this field. The most important of these outside influences in sculpture is that of the Chinese. As with the Chinese, Vietnamese sculpture often centers on statues in pagodas and other objects used in worship at home and other religious places. They show a preference for the four fabulous animals and the four seasons, just as the Chinese do.

Some evidence of Cham sculpture can still be seen in Vietnam. It is often typified by statues of women having wings and large breasts, quite different from Vietnamese sculpture.

Painting Visitors to Vietnam are well impressed by the sensitive artistry of Vietnamese painters, especially in the field of popular painting. Their work is very pleasing to the eye, with delicate forms and color combinations.

The art is a combination of Occidental and Oriental influences. An effort is being made by the National School of Fine Arts to bring these two forces together harmoniously. A new and different era for the Vietnamese painter may well be in the making.

The artists in South Vietnam today seem to be experimenting and a visit to the exhibitions often held in major cities may bring some surprising results. Painting is very popular among the Vietnamese and thousands of people turn out for exhibitions held almost weekly in Saigon.

There are many good artists in South Vietnam, and I have chosen a few from among them as representative of their contemporaries.

One well-known artist in Vietnam is Nguyen Tri Minh. He made a trip to the United States in 1963 and recorded his impressions of the places he visited on canvas, half in water color, half in oil. He is noted for the texture of his paintings, wh ch are considered to be simultaneously elegant and powerful. He considers himself as belonging to the "semiabstract expressionist school." He is married to another well-known artist, Truong Thi Thinh.

Another form of art popular in the country is the painting of scrolls and panels, with designs continuing from one to another. A leading artist in this field is Vi Hand. This work is generally considered to be "Chinese painting."

One original form of art practiced by Nguyen Van Lich and Dang Nhu Ho is the making of beautiful pictures from postage stamps and other pieces of colored paper. Their work was made public in January of 1964 for the first time, and critics said a new art form had been devised in Vietnam. A few of the critics called their work "handicrafts."

Music Until the end of the 19th century, the music played in Vietnam was regulated by certain laws administered by Hue court. Most of the laws were imported from China and limited the repertory of music to a few typical tunes which were used with certain rituals.

This lasted until approximately 1900 when musical amateurs introduced new innovations, changing the nature of music in the country.

The new repertory was divided into two classes: the dieu bac (allegro), northern tunes which are lively and cheerful, and dieu nam (lento), southern tunes which are listless and lamentful. Vietnamese musical artists are required to know these two classical repertories by heart, conforming to the tempo and times imposed for each different melody. Interpretation of these tunes may be carried out but they must remain to be recognizable.

A classical Vietnamese band includes a double-stringed guitar, a three-stringed guitar, a sixteen-stringed psaltery (don tranh), a single-stringed doc huyen, a rhythm-maker (song lang), and a two-stringed rovanastron (don co).

For the classical theater, other instruments including drums, gongs, trumpets, etc., are added, and they are used to stress the action on the stage, not to achieve harmony.

Many instruments have been imported from China, but there are a few instruments that are strictly Vietnamese. Among them are the following:

Don Doc Huyen or Don Bau

Of ancient origin, this one-stringed instrument can achieve tones considered superior to those of the Hawaiian guitar. Numerous sounds can be attained with the instrument, including that of the human voice. The sounds are made by pinching the string at set distances, while simultaneously the tautness is changed with the left hand on another part of the instrument.

Vo de Cam

This is a type of guitar made with a long handle placed into a rectangular, bottomless sound box. Only the top of the instrument is closed. There is a bridge on top supporting three strings which continue to pegs fixed at the top of the handle with eight finger boards.

Senh Tien

A most simple percussion instrument, the senh tien is made up of two pieces of wood attached by a hinge. On the top piece, which is shorter, copper coins are held in place. The musical sound is achieved by clapping the two pieces of wood together and the noise of the coins, which are allowed to move vertically, completes the unusual sound.

Music Today Young people in Vietnam today do not have the same intense interest in traditional music as their ancestors. Many of the elders lament that the young are only interested in the new popular music and do not care to learn the music which has been so popular in Vietnam's history.

Youngsters do not find the glamour in the traditional musical instruments that they like in the gleaming Western instruments. However, there are still those students who attend the music schools in the country to study traditional music. No doubt, many of them are there to please their parents. Those serious students of traditional music in the schools need more encouragement so that this art form in Vietnam will not be allowed to dwindle away. It would be in very poor condition today were it not for the new interest in the modern theater which uses traditional music to accompany the acting.

THEATER

THERE ARE three types of dramatic theater arts in Vietnam. They are the Hat Boi, Hat Cheo, and Cai Luong.

Hat Boi Classical Theater Hat Boi theater originated in China and was officially recognized there at king Han Vu De's court (140–86 B.C.). The Chinese evidently brought the art to Vietnam during their control of the country. Many Vietnamese do not like to admit to their culture being Chinese oriented and may argue this point emphasizing that in some Vietnamese productions, not a single Chinese tune or musical instrument is used. They say that Chinese elements of the art in Vietnam have almost disappeared.

In the early history of Hat Boi Theater in Vietnam, the participating artists were spurned by the Vietnamese elite. King Le Thanh Ton (1460–90) decreed that comedians, singers, and actors, sould not compete in the examinations given for places in the Mandarinate.

Later, the Emperor Tu Duc said, "Actors do not belong to the human kind." They were criticized as having bad morals. Today, this stigma no longer exists in Vietnam.

In the traditional Vietnamese theater, everything is kept as simple as possible. There is no stage scenery, curtain or special lighting effects. There is one entrance and exit to the stage for the artists. There is little or no furniture on the stage. If there is, it will have a symbolic meaning.

Convention plays an important role in Hat Boi. The actors are limited to a few exacting rules. There are many symbols used, and the audience generally knows them all, so that they participate to some extent in the understanding and feeling of the production.

Subjects are legendary and are almost superhuman; certainly they are not like the ordinary man on the street.

Even the use of makeup is regulated and an artist must conform to the dictates in the field. The features of the characters are revealed by their wrinkles, color of their makeup, beards, etc. In China, the mask is used more often than in Vietnam.

Characters are so much alike from one play to another that the audience can recognize them immediately. For instance, the strong and fearless knight always has a red face, Phoenix's eyes, and a long silky beard.

The beard has always played an important part in Hat Boi. It has different meanings, depending on how the actor handles it. Meditation, anger, worry, etc. are understood by the audience without confusion just by watching the actor finger his beard in a specific manner.

Whereas staging is rather dull without the use of many props, wardrobes are just the opposite. They are often so elaborate and magnificent that they cost a fortune.

Artists performing in Hat Boi always introduce the character they are portraying, when they first make their appearance on stage. They do this by reciting a Bach which is two lines with seven syllables in each. Normally, the characters are like superhuman creatures who get involved in grand adventures and always prove their moral greatness.

Some of the leading Hat Boi artists include Miss Thu Ba, Miss Le Tham, Miss Kim Cuong Phung Ha, and actors Nam Chau, Minh Chi, and Van Khoe.

Hat Cheo This particular form of the popular theatrical art is most favored in North Vietnam. It is a simplified version of the Hat Boi. Whereas Hat Boi is always a tragedy or deep drama, Hat Cheo also uses some comedy.

Cai Luong Modern Theatrical Troupes In addition to the classical theater, there are approximately 1,300 professional stage performers in 40 theatrical troupes throughout the country of South Vietnam. Their performances are well-liked by thousands of Vietnamese who turn out regularly to see the visiting entertainers. Many of them are idolized like movie stars of other countries. There are some who cause as much ruckus when they play in a Vietnamese town as rock and rollers do in the United States.

These Cai Luong troupes, which began in Vietnam in 1920, use comedy as well as tragedy. Their stories are more human and down-to-earth than the classical theater which extols traditional virtues.

Skilled musicians perform the background music which is limited to approximately 20 tunes each for sadness, anger, joy, and other emotions. Therefore, avid theatergoers can recognize the melody and popular ones cause a roar of applause each time they are played.

The actors and actresses usually begin their roles in a conversational tone. When the action of the play becomes more involved, they often speak as if they were reciting verse, and quite suddenly they may break into song.

The musical accompaniment, settings, extravagent costumes, lighting effects, and well-known actors and actresses, especially those with good voices, offer an exciting evening for a Vietnamese.

Many of the conservative Vietnamese fear that Cai Luong or the modern theater is dealing a death blow to the traditional Hat Boi theater in Vietnam.

MODERN ENTERTAINMENT

The Film Industry The film industry in Vietnam is still in its infancy, but is producing several movies yearly. They are generally low-budget, rather sensational movies geared to Vietnamese taste.

Most of the actors and actresses work only part-time and hold down other jobs as well. The actresses are considered to be among the most beautiful women in Vietnam.

One of the leading actresses is Kieu Chinh. She has appeared in the American movie, "Year of the Tiger," opposite actor Marshall Thompson.

Another Vietnamese beauty in the film business is Tham Thuy Hang, who often represents Vietnam at Asian film festivals.

Well-known Singers Vocalists in Vietnam are very popular and in the larger cities, often rotate from one supper club to another in one night, so a whole string of different singers may be heard while staying at one establishment.

Among the most popular is Bach Yen (white swallow), a well-known singer of ballads, folk, and love songs. She has travelled in the war-torn areas of Vietnam singing to the Vietnamese and American soldiers. She appeared on the Ed Sullivan show in the United States in 1965.

Other popular singers are Yen Vy, Lan Huong, Mary Linh, Ngoc Nhi, Tuy Phuong, and My Hinh. There are also a few popular male singers, but they are not so much in demand as the lovely girls.

LITERATURE

THE EARLIEST recorded poetry and prose was written by Buddhist bonzes who exchanged their writings with the poets in China. These writings were almost completely Chinese in form. Most of the Vietnamese forms were memorized in the spoken Vietnamese language and passed down orally through generations.

Later writers broke away from the strict Chinese characters and added some of their own combinations representing ideas and phonetizing the native language. This was called Chu Nom.

This enabled the writers and poets more latitude, and for the first time, to write down the prose and verse which had been used in the spoken language until this time. They were then able to break away from the Chinese influence.

With the advent of Quoc Ngu, the romanized version of the language, in the 17th century, the Vietnamese literary class was able to translate some of Europe's masterpieces into Vietnamese. In addition, this new language development enabled the Vietnamese to express themselves in literature.

Due to the closeness of Vietnamese life to nature and their pseudo-scientific beliefs, the poetic form has been the main form of their expression for hundreds of years. Since the beginning of the century, many talented poets have composed their sentiment and deeper feelings in the national language. These works are highly regarded and are frequently read on special occasions as indicative of the Vietnamese indigenous art form. Principal among these has been the works of Nguyen-Khac-Hieu, who was known as Tan-Da (1889–1939).

The most recent theme of Vietnamese literature and poetry centers on the theme of emancipation from the family cult and is evident in the writings of such moderns as Hoang-Ngoc Phach, Nhat-Linh, Khai-Hung, and Le-Van-Truong.

Poetry The Vietnamese people are very fond of poetry. Not only poets but everyday folk take any opportunity possible to make a rhyme. At times of great happiness or sorrow, the average Vietnamese may take pen in hand and vent his innermost feelings on paper. Poems have been passed down through generations, some of them not transcribed on paper. They vividly tell the history, customs and culture of the country.

The beauty of Vietnam's women has often been extolled in poetry. The habitual chewing of betel nut produces a blackening effect on the teeth until they appear as though they have been lacquered. In the past, such black teeth were an object of admiration, hence this excerpt from a poem.

Do you remember me when you go home
When I go home I remember your teeth
Shown while you're smiling
I would pay one hundred taels
For that smiling mouth
And one thousand taels
For that person having black teeth

Early marriage as explained in Chapter 6 was condemned by one victim in the following verse.

My mother was greedy for
A basket of steamed glutinous rice
A fat pork and Canh Hung taels
I told her to refuse
She mumbled and brought me in
Now my husband is short

And I am tall
Like a pair of unequal chopsticks

In addition to the poems written by the people, there are poets who employed a strict discipline in their work. One example of this is the eight line poem called the Bat Cu. In each of the eight lines there must be seven words or feet (a group of syllables marking a metrical unit in verse) which are monosyllabic. The pauses marking a rhythmic point of division must come after the fourth foot. The rhyme is the same throughout the poem and the tone of every word is fixed. The introduction is formed in the first two lines and the conclusions in the last two. The message of the poem, therefore, must be concentrated in the remaining four lines.

A 15th century emperor pondered his thought on the condition of mankind in such a poem, the conciseness of which is lost in translation.

I shudder whenever I think of existence
Sent into life, I go back to death
Intelligence, idiocy: joined together under nine feet of earth
Riches, poverty: a pot of rice cooking!
To struggle? Before my eyes, clouds dissolving
To suffer? Behind my body, very heavy mountains!
Vainly I question Heaven
Yet, I strive to live, listening out for Fate!

The most famous poem in Vietnam was written by Nguyen Du in the 18th century. He was often called the Revolutionary Poet. The epic narrative poem entitled, Kim Van Kieu, is so popular that it is known by virtually every Vietnamese, regardless of his status in life. It is considered the national poem.

Kim Van Kieu has 3,254 verses with 22,778 words which tell the story of an extraodinarily beautiful girl named Thuy Kieu. The girl, in order to save her family, gives up the man she loves to marry a rogue who leads her to prostitution. In the poem, she plays the roles of prostitute, student's mistress, servant, Buddhist nun, a victorious revolutionary's wife, and other characters. She undergoes ravishment, sacrifice, glory, and betrayal. Despite all of this, she managed to keep her soul intact. Hence, the main theme "The source of the Good lies in our hearts, and the heart, by itself, is worth three times more than talent."

Actually, the girl in the poem symbolizes the author, who was caught in the unfortunate politics during the decline of the Nguyen Dynasty to which he was attached by birth, and the Tay Son's who were claiming the throne. The beautiful girl, Thuy Kieu, and her fate was an analogy of Nguyen Du's.

Nguyen Du was of the Mandarin class and belonged to one of the most famous families of the Vietnamese aristocracy. He was born in 1765 and died in 1820. A long, narrow street in Saigon, near the Gia Long Palace, which houses the National Music School and other schools, is named for this famous author.

Prose Vietnamese prose first appeared in the Chinese language. Its quality was rather poor, but it is valuable for the wealth of information that it holds regarding Vietnamese customs and culture in that era. Nguyen-Trai was one of the first of these writers who phrased their thoughts in Chinese. He wrote the "Proclamations of the Emperor Le-Loi" and the first "Manual of Geography" among other famous works.

Beginning with the 13th century, several significant historical works were completed. They include: *The Historical Memories of the Great Viet* (1272), *A Historical Precis of Annam by Le Ta* (1323), *An Abbreviated History of Viet by Ly-Te-Xuyen* (1323); and the better known works published by each dynasty since 1272. They were called Annals.

Later significant contributions of Vietnamese literary forms in the Chinese language are the two great encyclopedias of Vietnam. The first is by Le-Qui-Don (1726–84). It provides critical commentaries on Chinese literature. The second is by Phan-Huy-Chu (1782–1840) which is considered to be an important source document for students of early Vietnamese history, geography, customs, and institutions.

Even though these minor works began to break away from the stilted Chinese form as early as the 16th century, it was not until the work of the Vietnamese poet Nguyen Du that we can detect a clear emergence of Vietnamese style.

CRAFTS

EVERYONE likes to take something home for himself and his family from a country, where he has been, usually an item unique to the country. Vietnam has an outstanding supply of such souvenirs.

In some handicrafts, similarity can be seen to those found

in China. This is only natural, since the Chinese dominated Vietnam at many different times during history, and their influence has been greatly felt in the artistic fields.

As other foreign powers have come along, the Vietnamese have formed new types of handicraft to suit them. For the French, the Vietnamese perfected the art of dainty, embroidered lingerie and clothing. When the Americans came to help the South Vietnamese in their fight against the communists, the enterprising Vietnamese learned to embroider jackets with crazy slogans on the back and to make footlockers out of old beer and softdrink cans. Some of the Americans were interested in having golf bags, shoes, handbags, etc. made out of elephant hide, and a new handicraft in the field of leather was begun.

The Vietnamese are great "copyists." All one has to do is show them a picture and they will duplicate it.

There are many fine handicrafts which are part native to Vietnam or were perfected to a fine art there. A few of the most important ones are discussed here. In addition to those who specialize in clothing and food techniques, Vietnamese craftsmen can generally be divided into nine categories:

1. Craftsmen who make cultural or religious objects
2. Wood and stone sculptors
3. Japanners (lacquer work)
4. Leather craftsmen
5. Craftsmen working on ivory, horn, and tortoise shell
6. Textile craftsmen—to include silk weavers, cotton and ramie jet weavers, basket-makers, sail-makers, etc.
7. Wood craftsmen—shipwrights, paper makers, printers, etc.

8. Ceramics craftsmen
9. Metal craftsmen

Vietnamese history indicates that craftsmen have been quite free. In the past, the Imperial Court in Hue protected craftsmen and sponsored state workshops in which only the best equipment and materials were furnished. The Court bought the best works including embroideries, inlaid works, engraved silver objects of art, lacquers, ivory objects, jewels, etc. They also sponsored the sale of the other items not bought by the Court.

Tools of Trade The tools used by Vietnamese craftsmen are usually quite simple and easy to make. Engineers have tried to improve upon some of them, only to find that they were the best to be had.

The wooden wedge is used in Vietnam where the screw and bolt is often used by Chinese craftsmen.

The wedge-press, cogwheel, shaft, paddle-wheel, easel, and level are in use almost universally in Vietnam.

Metal Craftsmen According to historical documents, techniques in metallurgy were developed in Vietnam during the first century before the birth of Christ. The substratum in North Vietnam was veined with gold, silver, iron, and tin.

One particular field of metal work, that of copper work, was begun in the reign of Tran-Thai-Ton (1225–58). A bonze, Khong-Lo, from Bac-Ninh province, began the craft in Vietnam. After his daily duties, he used to model clay into molds into which he poured molten copper. His objects were said to be as good as those imported from China.

Two other bonzes began to help him and he was able to make trays, vases, copper containers, bells, statues of Buddha, and other religious objects.

He was most elated by his success and returned home where he taught the craft to his fellow villagers. The practice spread to other villages and prosperity came to the makers of copper items. Upon his death, a temple was built to his memory in his home town.

Early Money Coin collectors are saddened that the gold Sapeks begun in Hanoi by Luu-Xuan-Tin in the 15th century are now extinct. Later, ordinary sapeks were moulded and cast, but not of the precious gold metal.

Luu-Xuan-Tin who lived during the reign of Le-Thanh-Ton (1460–97) was dissatisfied with the methods of barter used in commercial relations, and he thought of making a coin which could be used in exchange. He presented his idea to the king, who authorized him to start making the coins and gave him the capital he needed. Luu-Xuan-Tin began making gold and silver coins, but went to Hanoi trying to locate other suitable metals.

The king made Luu-Xuan-Tin the Minister of Finance and ordered that a temple be built to his memory in his home town of Chau-Khe.

Jewelers Jewelry is one thing that the French and Americans really get excited about in Vietnam. The gold used is usually 18 karat, but the natives prefer 24 karat, which has a more orange color. The goldsmiths are very talented and copy or fabricate any design you like. Labor is relatively cheap, cutting the cost of the finished article. The price of the gold fluctuates with the value of Vietnamese currency. Many natives take their earnings and buy gold or gold jewelry in case Vietnamese money should be devalued, the reason you see so many ordinary low-salaried people wearing gold bracelets and rings.

The goldsmith's tools in the beginning were quite crude, consisting of various hammers, gravers, and a small anvil. They used a horizontal bellows worked by a piston, which forced air onto a hearth made of fire-clay, filled with charcoal. Nowadays they have the help of gas flames.

There are three patrons of the goldsmith, Tran Hoa, Tran Dien, and Tran Dieu. They were three orphan brothers who lived in the reign of Ly-Nam-De (544–48).

Because of dire conditions in Vietnam, the three left for China, but lost their fortunes to thieves in Vietnam on the way. During one of the robberies, the brothers became separated. The two younger brothers managed to find one another, but lost all trace of their elder brother.

The two younger brothers went to work in a goldsmith's shop in China in Tan country and the elder brother found work as a goldsmith's assistant in Tuy country.

After three years of hard work, the elder brother had learned all of the secrets of the gold trade and asked to return to Vietnam to search for his two brothers.

When he returned to his village, he was told that his two brothers had been massacred by pirates. He went into deep mourning on their account and refused to leave Vietnam.

One day, the elder brother was amazed to see his two long lost brothers enter the village. After their first affectionate embraces, they asked each other what trades they had adopted. As it turned out, the eldest was skilled in the art of gold decorations while the younger ones well trained in working with precious metals. It was quite a coincidence that all three had found work in the gold field in China.

The three established their own goldsmith shop together and called it Kim-Hoang. Specializing in gem work of a subtle and exalted quality, they received numerous orders from the king and began to teach their craft to other people in their village.

When they died, a temple was built in their memory.

Pottery Some of the most famous pottery in Asia is found in Vietnam. A great deal comes from a school located at Bien-Hoa, a short distance from Saigon. There is also a noted pottery center near Hanoi.

One of the most popular pieces with foreigners are the large ceramic elephants, weighing over 50 pounds. Many an elephant, ceramic of course, has been tagged and shipped unwrapped through the military postal system to friends in the United States from American men in Vietnam.

Simple pottery has been known since antiquity. The Vietnamese, however, were not able to make large objects until a Chinese visitor, who was an expert in the field, offered to show some natives how to make a large water storage pot when he saw that the natives drank water from the streams.

Only one Vietnamese responded to his offer of instruction. His name was Truong-Trung-Ai. It took him three months to learn how to do some of the complicated tasks his Chinese instructor taught him. When he finally learned, he offered the Chinese 20 gold bars as a reward.

Truong-Trung-Ai made constant progress in the art and

began to show his fellow villagers how to do the work.

Two temples were built in Vietnam in honor of famous potters. One was dedicated to the Chinese man, Hoang-Quang-Hung, who originally taught the art to the Vietnamese and the other to his student, Troung-Trung-Ai. These temples are still in existence.

Lacquer Work The handicraft that interests visitors to Vietnam more than any other is the beautiful lacquer work.

The people of Vietnam have worked with lacquer for centuries, but the craft reached its fullest development during the reign of Le-Thanh-Ton (1443–60).

Up to this time, Vietnamese craftsmen had not been able to duplicate the lacquer work of the Chinese, as their decorations of gold and silver would not affix themselves to the wood because of lack of drying. Most of the workers in lacquer lost heart, except for one by the name of Tran-Truong-Cong, who asked the king to send him to China to find the secret of the Chinese process.

In China, he succeeded in mastering the process and learning the secret (which was to apply a layer of kaolin and gum before applying the lacquer to the wood). Due to his success, a temple was built in his village in his honor.

Embroidery Because of the Vietnamese trait of patience and artistry, embroidery is one of their specialties. Their works are very rich, often done with gold and silver threads.

In olden days, silk embroideries were especially made to

honor important people or to illustrate religious concepts. Also, tales from Vietnamese mythology were illustrated in silk embroideries.

The founder of embroidery was Le-Cong-Huanh who was sent by King Le-Chieu-Ton (1516–27) to China to look for new trades which would help the economic situation in Vietnam. He stayed in China for 14 years before bringing back embroidery to the Vietnamese people. He first introduced it to his home town, Ha-Dong, which became famous for its work and sewed special royal embroideries.

OTHER SPECIAL CRAFTS

Horn, Ivory, and Tortoise Shell Vietnamese craftsmen are especially adept at engraving horn and ivory. A special skill is converting the ordinary turtle's shell into a gleaming, smooth work of art. It is a long intricate process. Popular items are jewelery boxes, sunglasses, bracelets, necklaces, cigarette cases, etc.

Leather Work Vietnamese people first learned about leather work from Nguyen Thoi Trung who is the patron of shoemakers and tanners. He also invented a deodorant for bad-smelling hides. Today, one of the favorite streets for foreigners in Saigon is Le-Thanh-Ton Street, better known as "shoe street" where large numbers of shoe-makers and leather craftsmen sell their wares. They specialize in shoes, brief cases, golf bags, pistol holsters, and special objects made of leather. Quality is generally good, but delivery is slow.

Fans, Blinds, and Mats There were two kinds of fans in Vietnam in the past. Large fixed ones were made of feathers and reserved for high dignitaries of the court. There were also small ones, made of ivory, horn, or bamboo. The smaller ones are a specialty in shops in Vietnam today.

Blind-makers prepare elaborately decorated blinds out of bamboo, cotton string, varnishes, colouring, and starch paste. Mat makers use the reeds which flourish along the lengthy shoreline of the China Sea. Most of the items are used by the Vietnamese in their homes.

Inlaying Other favorite souvenirs are articles made with inlaid mother of pearl and eggshell. Nguyen Kim began this Vietnamese specialty, and schools for inlayers are found throughout the country. The Vietnamese like the inlaid, ornate furniture in their homes, but it is often quite expensive. Inlay work was known in Vietnam before the Christian era. One of the loveliest of the inlaid mother of pearl souvenirs are four plaques representing the seasons of the year.

CHAPTER 8

HEALTH AND WELFARE

ONE ONLY has to pass a store that sells caskets in Vietnam to see that death takes more than its normal toll in this little country. Unfortunately, children's caskets outnumber the adult by a considerably large ratio.

As in most of the under-developed nations, the major problem in Vietnam is communicable disease. This is primarily due to the fact that neither adequate preventive nor therapeutic health measures have been fully developed. Illnesses which take an alarming toll are malaria, other insect borne diseases, tuberculosis, intestinal diseases, diphtheria, whooping cough, measles, plague, cholera, typhoid, etc.

Due to the war and its effect on civilians, social welfare also presents a grave problem.

Origin of Medicine The first doctor in Vietnam was Tue-Thin, a bonze, who lived during the 10th century. Early in his life, he studied to be a teacher.

King Dinh-Tien-Goang wanted to make him a court mandarin, but Tue-Tinh refused because he consulted the Book of Prophecies and learned that the Dinh Dynasty was to be only a transient one.

He told the king that he wanted only to be a good teacher. When the king insisted that he accept, he had to flee to another province from his home. Angered, the king sent an expeditionary force to look for Tue-Tinh, but by this time the bonze had escaped to China. He settled at the Pagoda of Vanphuc which was called the "land of Confucius."

One day the bonzes of this pagoda were visited by Duong-Quang-Thanh, the most celebrated doctor in China at that time. He was very impressed with the bonze Tue-Tinh, and he offered to teach him the art of medicine.

Tue-Tinh gratefully accepted and studied under the master of medicine for ten years. He was said to be an even greater doctor after ten years than his teacher.

The bonze felt the desire to go home again and asked his teacher for permission and it was granted. When he got back to Vietnam, he found that the Dinh Dynasty had, indeed, ended as the prophecy said, and Le was now the king.

Tue-Tinh took up the practice of medicine in the old pagoda in Hong-Van, was so versed that he became famous and was soon overwhelmed by the number of his patients. He took in students, who in turn became well-known.

King Le-Trung-Ton was cared for and healed by Tue-Tinh at one time when there was little hope for the king's recovery. Later, when Tue-Tinh died, the king ordered that an official cult be instituted in his memory and that a temple be erected.

Tue-Tinh was the first man to bring medicine to Vietnam

on a national basis. He did a great deal of research and wrote his observations in a book written entirely by hand, *Nam-Duoc* (Medicines of the South).

Medicine Today At the present time in South Vietnam, there is only one graduate physician for approximately 28,000 people in the country. This is further complicated by the fact that the majority of the physicians available are in the army.

To alleviate the shortage, other Vietnamese have gone into their own business, labeling themselves as "bac-si" or "doctor." Westerners refer to them as "quacks," but many of these herb doctors are highly respected by the Vietnamese, the literate as well as the illiterate.

Sometimes it is a hard decision for a Vietnamese to make when he must decide whether to use Western methods or Oriental drugs. If it is an emergency, they will usually take Western medicine. If they are not in a hurry, they generally prefer Eastern concoctions which they believe to be slower, but surer.

There are two types of drug stores in Vietnam. The traditional Oriental shop has one or two large chests with hundreds of tiny drawers containing medicaments. At the cashier's counter, there is a brass mortar and a pig-iron grinder. This, plus the abacus, is all the equipment needed for preparing remedies.

The Occidental type, or Western pharmacy, on the other hand, has shelves loaded down with numerous little bottles and boxes. Most of the medicines are already prepared.

Though the appearances are different, in some circumstances the medications are very similar. For instance, both types of pharmacies stock quinine for malaria, artemisia for backache, etc. Some Eastern medicines have been accepted by Western experts as "law."

While the Western field of medicine is constantly improving, the Occidental one has not changed in thousands of years.

For centuries, Oriental practitioners have been looked upon as altruistic scholars. There are very few textbooks on traditional therapy and most of the physicians have to improve their knowledge by experience and usually earn their reputation after years of practice.

Vietnamese medicine stems from Chinese therapy of centuries ago. The best-known figure in traditional medicine is Hai-Thuong-Lan-Ong (Le Huu Chan) from North Vietnam. He wrote a complete series of medical books in the 16th century which are followed today by Oriental practitioners.

Theory of Oriental Medicine

According to traditional medical theory, the human body includes five main internal organs: heart, liver, spleen, lungs, and kidneys, plus six secondary viscera. Besides having a close connection with each other, these organs are also considered closely related with the five senses represented by the tongue, nose, ears, eyes, and mouth. Five juices: sweat, urine, sputum, saliva, and tears; the five tastes: salty, bitter, hot, sour, and sweet; the five colors: red, blue, black, white, and yellow; and five types of weather: hot, cold, windy, dry, and humid, all play an important role in the theory. In addition, the body is considered to undergo the influence of five natural elements that surround it, metal, wood, water, fire, and earth, plus the five directions of north, south, east, west, and center.

The Oriental doctor practicing traditional medicine also

believes in the concept of a close connection between the universe and the human body. Therefore, he must be versed in many sciences, such as physics, mathematics, astronomy, and astrology.

By tradition, the physician should be altruistic and not out to earn a lot of money. Though many have become wealthy, many are content to live modestly, and often treat the sick free of charge.

Doctors practicing traditional medicine should not be confused with the real "quacks" giving medical advice on street corners and selling their wares. Unfortunately, many Vietnamese put their trust in these "overnight" doctors and pay out large sums of money to them. Though Westerners may frown on the doctor practicing traditional medicine, there is a vast difference in their methods of practice and these street corner merchants.

A Few Important Statistics

In all of South Vietnam, there are approximately:

800 physicians, 500 of whom are in the Armed Forces
75 dentists
380 pharmacists (Western oriented)
1,200 midwives
3,100 nurses at various levels, including non-graduates
4 sanitary engineers
140 sanitary agents
3,500 village health workers

The Vietnamese government's Department of Health conducts the medical program in South Vietnam. It is responsible for technical direction to almost all of the hospitals in the country. A few private institutions, mostly in Saigon, are excepted.

The Department of Health maintains training schools for nurses, midwives, and auxiliary health personnel. A typical provincial health department will have a hospital with 100–300 beds and supervises a varying number of district infirmary-maternities and health stations. All of them are understaffed, and many of the smaller units are run by midwives and nurses. An American joke that is only too true is that "semi-private" in a Vietnamese hospital means two in a single bed.

What is Being Done to Help The major help for South Vietnam's medical problems is now coming from the United States. Of the various United States sources, the main help comes from the American government aid program.

The Agency for International Development (AID) program has worked toward expansion and improvement of the medical college in Saigon. Plans are in effect which will bring 150 new graduate physicians into practice each year beginning with 1966. U.S. aid has also assisted in the building a new medical school at the University of Saigon, including a school of dentistry a biochemical laboratory, a library, and an auditorium.

An extensive effort to cope with the predominant disease conditions by developing and enlarging upon the basic health facilities in Vietnam by the government, is being supplemented with help from the AID program. American teachers have been supplied to the Vietnamese government until more Vietnamese can be trained both at home and abroad.

A Department of Preventive Medicine has been established with malaria eradication as one of its principal goals. The Rural Health Program trains auxiliary health personnel to perform as health workers in the countryside. Though their work is simple, it is much needed and can often save hundreds of villagers' lives. For instance, a child in Vietnam may lose his sight because of the lack of a simple antibiotic treatment. There are thousands of blind people in the country whose sight could have been saved with this simple treatment. The Rural Health workers are trained to recognize such diseases and treat them. The U.S. Army Special Forces also work as medical cadre in remote outposts. In recent months other military personnel have joined in this work, holding sick call along with their military operations.

Health films are now presented and lectures are given throughout the country in an attempt to educate the people in the ways of sanitation and good health.

Surgical teams provided by the United States, Korea, the Philippines, Australia, New Zealand, Italy, and Taiwan, are now performing surgery in the provinces.

"Project Vietnam," the result of President Johnson's call for medical help in June of 1965 is also in effect. The program calls for $500,000 grant aid from the Agency for International Development to be administered by the People to People Health Foundation. It is a 3 year plan to help with increased civilian casualties on account of the war. Twenty American doctors will serve for 90 or more days in hospitals in Vietnam on a rotating basis under the program. Response from medical personnel in the United States has been quite good.

There are two nursing education centers in South Vietnam.

One is in Saigon and the other 600 miles north in Hue. More dormitories and class rooms have been constructed. Other assistant nurse programs have been improved.

Other Agencies Many private agencies have lent aid in the medical field in Vietnam. There are far too many to enumerate here, but a few of the best-known include the following:

The Care-Medico program has sponsored one-month tours by American plastic surgeons, orthopedic surgeons, obstetricians, gynecologists, and general surgeons in the medical facilities for several years. The physicians pay their own expenses to Vietnam and donate their time. In addition, Project HOPE maintains a fulltime Orthopedic Clinic in Saigon with an American surgeon in residence.

American heart specialists have made periodic visits performing operations and demonstrating to medical personnel the latest techniques to treat heart diseases.

The United Nations Childrens' Fund has worked closely with the South Vietnamese government in implementing laboratory services, nutrition courses, and leprosy control. They have also provided equipment for the creation of three mobile teams, including laboratory equipment, drugs, and vehicles. Funds have been contributed for a maternal and child health center, tuberculosis control and community education programs.

American Magic Men Often the things that people remember most, no matter where they live, are the events that are quick and dramatic. In Vietnam, one group of Americans came in the height of a cholera epidemic and quickly earned the reputation among those witnessing their work as being the American Magic Men.

During this major epidemic, the U.S. Navy applied its latest cholera techniques, helping to save thousands of lives. Captain Robert A. Phillips was the Commanding Officer of the first team to arrive. He is credited as being one of the major "inventors" of the successful cholera treatment which is now being accepted around the world.

Basically, the treatment is an effort to replace fluids which have been lost as a result of diarrhea. The antidote consist of infusions of saline solutions and sodium bicarbonate. Rapid infusions and constant nursing care are vital to the treatment.

As a witness to this terrifying disease and having seen the patients brought into hospitals in comatose states with little hope of survival, I, along with the Vietnamese, attest to the magic qualities of Captain Phillips and his men during their stay in Vietnam.

The Little Helpers There have been hundreds of people, including Vietnamese, Americans, and French, who have worked quietly for their fellow man in Vietnam, without any thought of recognition or payment. Now, there are more coming from other friendly countries. Though they may despair at times because of the size of their chosen task their efforts are greatly appreciated by the individual Vietnamese they have helped. Their work is generally done in off-duty hours and there are no headlines proclaiming their good work. People like these are making a contribution that cannot be measured in dollar marks or words and certainly deserve the admiration of their fellow man.

SOCIAL WELFARE

Because of the war in South Vietnam, social welfare, for the most part is in a state of chaos. Here again, many voluntary agencies are assisting. Some of them include: CARE, Foster Parents Plan, Catholic Relief, Oxford Committee for Famine Relief, International Voluntary Service, Belgian Caritas Organization, The Red Cross, and The Asia Foundation. The Vietnamese government organizations and those from official American agencies continue their work under the worst possible conditions.

There are a few traditional social organizations which play an important role in Vietnamese rural villages where most of the people live. Some of these organizations have remained unchanged for several hundred years. They still function where any degree of peaceful living can be maintained. They include:

Religious Womens' Association "Hoi Chu Ba" If a village has a Buddhist pagoda, it will more than likely have a Buddhist Old Womens' Association. It is an organization for women at least fifty years of age or older. A few women who are widows in their late forties are also accepted.

These women are usually free of household cares because they are older and their children are grown. Normally, they are being supported by their children financially, so they are free to join the association. The old women try to go to the Pagoda each evening and study Buddhism and pray for the salvation of their souls.

They engage in welfare activities and also go to homes

where a death occurs to pray for the deceased and help the family.

Professional Guilds "Hoi Bach Nghe" In the past, most villages have been relatively economically independent. Foods, building materials, etc. are local products and every village usually has its own carpenters, blacksmiths, painters, masons, etc. Each trade has its own guild.

The guilds work at improving skills and also promote mutual friendship and help when in need. Gifts and cash are given to members on such occasions as marriage, child birth, and death. Needy or extremely large families are sometimes helped on a regular basis.

The group often has an investment club financed by the dues collected. These profits are distributed yearly among the members. A few of these guilds do not have dues. Instead, wealthy members contribute funds when the organization is set up.

Mutual Aid Societies If a member of a Mutual Aid Society is in need of funds for a funeral, wedding, special building project, etc. he applies to the chairman of the society. The chairman goes to other members and collects a sum of money as specified in the regulations and gives it to the person in need. In the case of death, members of the society help the bereaved family and dress in mourning attire and accompany the burial party to the cemetery.

Relief Fund The Emperor Tu-Duc (1847–83) declared that a relief fund would be set up in every village in the land. Farmers would contribute rice based on the acreage they cultivated. The relief fund is supposed to be closely regulated, with officers making spot checks and accounting for funds and rice. In the event of a flood or other disaster, the rice is distributed to needy people.

Other Organizations There are many other such organizations in the villages. But those described above seem to be the most popular, with each succeeding foreign influence; i.e., the French and the Americans, new institutions are established in an effort to keep up with the changing times.

CHAPTER 9

AGRICULTURE, FISHERY, INDUSTRY

South Vietnam is the rice-bowl of the country formerly known as Vietnam, with North Vietnam being noted for its industrial complexes. With the division of the country in 1955, both sides suffered.

The North was left without agricultural products formerly available from the South and famines have occurred. The South, on the other hand, was left with little or no industry. With the help of the United States Aid Program, and loans from other friendly countries, the government of South Vietnam has attempted to build a new line of industries to partially meet the country's needs.

Of the two, North Vietnam has suffered the most from their lack of agricultural products, and this may well be one of the driving reasons behind the insurgency. They desperately need the rice bowl of the South.

Latest figures for North Vietnam's exports and imports are

not available, so this chapter will deal only with the southern half of Vietnam.

Major Imports and Supplies The United States' commercial firms are the biggest suppliers to South Vietnam. In addition to the Agency for International Development (AID) program, the largest amounts of paid imports came from the United States. Others at the top of the list include France, Nationalist China, Japan, and Indonesia.

Major imported items include iron and steel products, machinery and equipment, yarns for the local textile industry, petroleum products, fertilizer, and prefabricated parts for assembly in Vietnam of such items as small motor vehicles, watches, clocks, transistor radios, etc.

Main Buyers of Vietnam Products Contrasting to the sale of products to Vietnam, the United States buys very little from the country. The top buyers from South Vietnam are France, Malaysia, and Philippines, West Germany and Great Britain (in descending order of value).

Four Main Exports Rubber and rice bounce back and forth from first to second place periodically as the two major exports. Tea ranks third and an unusual product is fourth—duck feathers. Almost 1000 tons of the downy product are exported annually, mostly to West Germany. In 1965 the Viet-Cong insurgency took its toll on the ability of South Vietnam to keep up its rising trend in exports. For the first time in recent years, it was necessary to import rice from the United States due to the inability to get the country's huge rice crop to market within the confines of South Vietnam. With the new American emphasis in the country, it is anticipated that exports will race back to their previous improved level and make even more progress.

AGRICULTURE

SOUTH VIETNAM is basically a country of agriculture. Four-fifths of its population work in its pursuit. The two most important crops are those of rice and rubber.

Rice Exports in an average year are around 250,000 metric tons, valued at approximately 25 million dollars. In 1965, the figure suddenly dropped due to the Viet-Cong insurgency. The figure quoted here for an average year could be even higher were it not for the communists who make transportation difficult, if not impossible in many cases. Often, rice is burned because of the inability to get it safely to market, and to deny its use to the Viet-Cong.

Rice is grown in a major portion of South Vietnam with the principal production area in the Mekong River Delta. Rice and fish are the principal foods in the Vietnamese diet.

Rubber Vietnam has been the fifth largest rubber producing area in the world. There has been some decline in the value of the rubber exported, due to the lower world rubber prices, and also because of Viet-Cong interference. The export value of rubber runs to approximately 30 million dollars per year at the present time. The French own most of the rubber plantations and are often forced to pay taxes to the Viet-Cong to be spared from their harassement.

Tea Vietnam's tea exports have increased steadily since 1960 with the latest figure showing an export of 2,000 tons in one year. Most of the tea exported is black tea, and the main purchasers are the United Kingdom and France. Green tea is consumed locally and only a small amount is exported. Tea production could be increased greatly, as the Rural Affairs Department in Vietnam reports that there are thousands of available acres in the Highlands which are suitable for tea production.

Duck Feathers One of the most unusual industries is that of the production of duck feathers which are the fourth largest export of South Vietnam. The raw material, that of the ducks, is locally produced. Duck is well-liked for eating, and the feathers and down are a financial bonus in Vietnam's economy.

Other Agricultural Products In addition to these two major crops, an intensive effort is being made, with the help of the United States, to diversify and improve the production of other agricultural products. It is planned that these new and improved areas of crop production will help satisfy local needs and allow for exportation of many items.

Some of them are:

CACAO

Vietnam is ideally suited for this crop and could be one

of the larger exporters of the world's cacao supply to be used for making cocoa and chocolate. An American AID project, begun in 1959 with the distribution of 8,000 cacao plants, is progressing fairly well, despite the insurgency.

Coconut

Production is ample to meet the country's needs, but it is now being increased in order to have more of the product available for export. It is an item with high nutritive value, said to be the same as rice, and can be used in making soap, candles, and margarine.

Coffee

Vietnam receives a higher coffee bean yield per acre of land than do other coffee producing countries in the world. Since the Vietnamese do not drink much coffee, most of it is exported. West Germany is the largest purchaser. Coffee was first planted in Vietnam in 1885 and South Vietnam now produces almost 4,000 tons annually. Most of it is grown in the Highlands.

Duck Eggs

Exported in large numbers to other Asian countries and also well-liked by the Vietnamese in their diet. They especially like partially hatched duck eggs. These are sold on the street in the cities and towns.

Forestry

The valuable resource of forestry is for the most part unusable due to the Viet-Cong control of wooded areas. Forest stands cover almost two and one-half million acres of South Vietnam. Approximately 85 per cent of these woods are classified as hardwoods. The remaining trees are mostly mangrove, pine, bamboo, and other related species. Pine trees are found primarily around Dalat and a two and three leaf pine is available. Mangrove trees that grow along the coasts south of Ca-Mau yield a high grade charcoal.

Kenaf Fibre

Primarily grown in the highlands or the mountain area of Vietnam. It is very good for making gunny sacks. Vietnam is the third largest world supplier of this product. The U.S. Aid program has helped develop this industry to a greater extent with improved methods and a better seed from El Salvador.

Lacquer

Lacquer has always been a prized export from Vietnam in the foreign market. Most of it came from North Vietnam, but experiments have shown that lacquer bearing trees can be grown with amazing success in the Highlands of South Vietnam.

Palm Oil

Since this oil does not become rancid and can be used for making margarine which does not require refrigeration, it is considered an ideal product in Vietnam. It has a higher vitamin and mineral content than coconut oil and is preferred for cooking. In addition, it can be used in the manufacture of soap, glycerine, and candles. The product is exported, though not on a large scale at the present time beause of the war's effect on production.

Peanuts

This is a quick growing crop which means money in the pocket for the farmer. It is mainly grown in the hilly areas and is one of the farmer's most important cash crops. Export of the item has been established.

Sea Swallow's Nests

A large number of these nests are used domestically and exported from the country. Not only are they well-liked for their gourment flavor, they are also sought for medicinal purposes. The Emperor Minh-Mang, who had over 150 children, credited his extraordinary virility to eating sea-swallow's nests. In addition to the nests, traditional medical practitioners use the bird's body and wastes eliminated from their body in making oriental medicines. Vietnam is a most favorable habitat for the sea swallow.

Sugar

New sugar mills, built by the Japanese and their investment capital, are scheduled to begin production on a large scale in 1967. Sugar cane can easily be grown in Vietnam but production has never met the needs of the country. Consequently, large amounts have to be imported each year, causing a drain on foreign currency. Efforts are being made to bring the production up to the needs required. In times of peace, Vietnam could become one of the leading sugar producers in the world.

Tobacco

Production of this popular item is increasing and there are firms from other countries working in Vietnam on its production and export. In addition, the tobacco produced is satisfactory to the local requirements, except for those Vietnamese with more sophisticated tastes who insist on smoking imported brands.

OTHER FOOD PRODUCE

Vegetables and Fruits Practically all of the vegetables and fruits grown are consumed within the country, especially the highly perishable types. Bananas and avocados are exported in fairly large quantities, however, when in season, mangoes and papaya are also exported. In addition, some commercial firms are producing meat tenderizer made from Vietnam's papayas. The fruits and vegetables in Vietnam are superb, especially those grown in and around the city of Dalat. An unusual feature there is that the crops grow throughout the year and the land is rarely left unused. Various fruits and vegetables are grown at different times during the year on the same land.

Dairy Production This is one area that is far behind the need for the products. Both Australia and the United States have participated in programs to develop dairy production in Vietnam. The supply is so inferior to the demand that condensed milk is often rationed in the country.

Livestock Improvement in this area has been brought about by US government assistance and a Vietnamese sponsored program aimed at eradicating disease in livestock through vaccination. Superior results have been obtained in the field of hog raising. Hog raising is a big business for the small farmer and in 1965 it was officially estimated that under the accelerated program there was now one hog per each four citizens in South Vietnam. Beef consumption is on the rise, a different trend from the past when many people refrained from eating it.

Spices Cinnamon is an important dollar export in Vietnam. It has also been very important to certain tribes in the Highlands who have benefited economically from the sale of cinnamon. Pepper production is still more or less in the experimental stages in Vietnam, except for the area called Haut-Donnai.

FISHERY

SOUTH VIETNAM's coastal area of approximately 1,260 miles is literally full of shrimp and crayfish, and over 50 species of fish which are of commercial value. There are also more than 200 other varieties of fish which are not of commercial value but are consumed by the local population. In addition to the coastal waters, there are numerous rivers and canals which hold a considerable supply of fish.

Commercial fishing has rapidly improved in the last few years due to a Vietnamese Government sponsored program supported by US which accomplished the following: modernized and motorized the fishing fleet; constructed fish landings, including pier, market, and parking space; built cold-storage facilities, developed fishery cooperatives through which members could obtain loans for equipment; and conducted experimental work in fish rearing.

An extensive pond-rearing program has helped to increase the fresh-water catch, and the salt-water catch is greater because fishermen can go further in their motorized crafts. Over 10,000 of Vietnam's 39,000 fishing junks were motorized by the end of 1964.

Fish-finding devices purchased by the Vietnamese Fisheries

Directorate have paid for themselves many times over by locating large concentrations of fish which has lead to greater domestic and export sales.

Traditional fishing nets are being discarded by even the oldest and most experienced fishermen in Vietnam as they have seen that they can increase their catch as much as 250% by using nylon nets.

A considerable portion of the fish catch is used to make the local sauce so popular with the natives. It is called "Nuoc-Mam." The Vietnamese use it even more often than Americans use catsup. It is part of their everyday diet and comes in many different qualities.

Americans often complain of the smell of nuoc-mam as it seems to linger in the air long after dinner-time in Vietnamese neighborhoods.

How Nuoc-Mam is Made

The fish is highly salted and placed in vats where it is compressed for four month to one year. As it ages, bacteria causes fermentation and the smell to an American is interpreted as "spoiled fish." The juice is drained off the vat and bottled. This is nuoc-mam.

Nuoc-mam is rich in acids, minerals, and vitamins. A by-product of the fish residue in the manufacture of nuoc-mam has been found to be an excellent fertilizer for rice and vegetable products. Another by-product is the extraction of sardine oil for use in oil-burning lamps, soap manufacture, paints, lubrication of small motors, and tanning of hides.

The Oceanography Institute in Nha-Trang has done most of the research which has been responsible for the vast improvement in Vietnam's fishing industry.

Shrimp They are found in great abundance in Vietnam and have a delicate flavor. Plans were underway to export them in tremendous amounts, but some technical difficulties regarding preparation and refrigeration have not been completely solved. Some frozen and dried shrimp are being exported at this time, but not near the possible potential.

INDUSTRY

WHEN THE country of Vietnam was divided in 1954, the South had virtually no industry and the economy was almost completely agricultural.

A new and rapidly growing industrial base is in operation with plans for more to come in the future. All of this has been accomplished despite the warfare going on.

On the whole, the Viet-Cong have done little to destroy what is being built in the industrial complex. Perhaps they believe it will be for their use in the future should they gain control of South Vietnam. In view of the strong American stand in the country, it would not be surprising to see the communists begin to try to wreck the progress that has already been made.

Much of the development in South Vietnam has been accomplished with the help and financial assistance of the United States Aid Program. Private industries and investors have also promoted the country's industrial development.

INDUSTRIAL DEVELOPMENT

Power A drastic shortage of power has hampered Vietnam's industrial development. Most of Vietnam's rural areas have no electric power except that provided by gasoline generators. The oil lamp and the candle are still the sources of light today in these communities as they have been for generations.

Fifteen privately-owned companies have supplied the power available in South Vietnam's major cities until this time. The gross deficiency has ended, however, in most urban areas with the completion of the 44 million dollar Danhim Power Plant, built mainly with Japanese Reparation Funds, and the An Hoa Nong Son industrial complex thermal plant, financed jointly by France and West Germany.

The An Hoa Nong Son plant produces 20,000 KW and the Danhim (or Da-Nhim) plant will have an eventual capacity of 500,000 KW hours.

Nuclear Research The Triga nuclear reactor, situated in the city of Dalat, 145 miles northeast of Saigon, is the first of this concept in research reactors to be put to use in Southeast Asia.

The reactor went into operation in February 1963 and is used for the production of electricity. In addition, research in other peaceful uses of nuclear power is conducted at the center.

The financing was arranged by a $350,000 "Atoms for Peace" grant from the United States government.

Scientists are utilizing the facilities to study ways to guard man's health and to provide more abundant food crops.

The Triga Mark II self-regulating reactor was built and installed at Dalat by the General Atomic Division of the General Dynamics Corporation of San Diego, California.

Miscellaneous Power Sources The US Aid program has introduced simple windmills as a means of power for pumping water for irrigation. This was previously a foot-pumping operation which took the farmer away from his other work.

Windmills are also used to generate power to charge batteries, which are in turn used to power small necessities, such as village alarm systems, small radio communication outfits, etc.

Water The construction of the 26 million dollar water supply system will soon be completed at Thu Duc, near Saigon. There will also be a treatment plant which will help in the fight against water-borne diseases so prevalent in the area serviced. It will be more than ample for Saigon's water needs and the new industrial complexes in the area. A new distribution system including 45,000 meters of cast-iron pipes is also included in the project.

Transportation There has always been a lack of adequate transportation in the country which has hampered progress and development in many fields. The most critical need is for a good highway system for fast and cheap transportation of people and merchandise.

The Viet-Cong have made matters worse by sabotaging the available roads. The re-building of these roads is one of the leading tasks of the Vietnam government with the help of the U.S. military and economic programs.

An example of what can be accomplished is the beautiful 20 mile four-lane highway leading from Saigon to Bien-Hoa. It was financed by a 35 million dollar grant from US Aid and approximately one-half million dollars paid by the Vietnamese government to property owners along the road's path. It connects Saigon with the new industrial complexes being developed at Thu-Duc. As a result of the highway, many other new industries have sprung up along the side of the highway.

Railroads The government of the country owns the trans-Vietnam Railway, 1,337 kilometers in length. Movement of passengers and cargo is long, tedious and extremely risky. Between 1961 and 1964, there were 795 sabotage cases with 16 railmen killed and 128 injured. Despite this situation, professional train men stick to their jobs.

Old rolling stock is being replaced in a modernization program. A good portion of this is being financed through a seven and a half-million dollar loan fund between the U.S. and Vietnam.

Air Transportation Air Vietnam is the only scheduled airline operating within the country. The importance of this airline has increased because of the Viet-Cong agitation along the roads, railways, and waterways.

Water Transportation Water lanes via rivers and canals are an important feature in Vietnam's transportation system, and is confined mainly to the Mekong delta. Over 85% of the delta's produce reaches Saigon by water. The cost of moving goods in this manner is two-thirds less than it would be by road. Over 150,000 people make their living in the water transportation industry.

A government sponsored dredging program for more and better canals is in progress. Part of this is financed by the US Aid Mission.

The Viet-Cong have also made the canals one of their targets as well as a method of transporting their own goods. River patrols check hundreds of craft every day, but it is near to impossible to check them all.

New Industrial Complexes Work has begun on the construction of the largest industrial project in South Vietnam. Twelve factories will be set up around the Nong-Son Coal Mine on the Thu-Bon River near Da-Nang. The complex will produce fertilizer, cement, paper pulp, dry ice for fisheries, glass, and electric power. The main source of raw material will be the anthracite from the Nong-Son Coal Mine, with an estimated production of 200,000 tons a year by 1966.

The location offers a port within 40 miles and natural resources such as magnetite, haematite, limonite, gold, copper, lead, graphite, and tin can be exploited. Manpower is also abundant in the area.

The most important dividend from the project will be the saving of foreign exchange now spent to import fertilizer and coal which is used in the production of electric power.

Another industrial complex is also in production at Thu-Duc near Saigon.

OTHER INDUSTRIES BEING DEVELOPED

Textiles One of the most rapid and intensive fields of development has been in textiles with new, modern factories with the best equipment now producing 90% of the country's requirements for cloth. There are now over 100,000 spindles and 3,000 looms in operation in South Vietnam. Over 40 million pounds of US surplus cotton is processed annually. In 1963, Vietnam shifted from importing to exporting silk, a smaller but equally dramatic phase of the textile industry.

Plastics There was no plastic production in South Vietnam in 1955 when the two countries were divided, but today's production covers the country's requirements.

Paper Two new paper mills have been built near Biet-Hoa which is a short distance from Saigon. The country is within reach of satisfying its needs in a few years. At the present time, there is still a shortage of newsprint and Saigon's numerous newspapers often complain of the shortage. Paper products totalling 17,000 tons were produced in 1964.

Rubber Over 800,000 bicycle tires were produced in the south in 1964. Factories are being planned for the manufacture of car and truck tires. Rubber soles for shoes are being produced now in large quantities.

Batteries and Light Bulbs Almost one million flashlight batteries are being produced annually and car batteries are also in production. Sufficient light bulbs for the country are being produced.

Other Industries Cement, ceramic products, aluminum ware, glassware, jute and "kenaf" bag manufacturing, pencil manufacture, pharmaceuticals, toilet articles, and wood products are some of the other industries which are being developed.

The largest industrial firms produce beer and soft drinks, electric power, matches, scooters and cycles, cigarettes, printed materials, ironware, metalware, rubber products, "nuoc-mam," and furniture.

Handicraft industries are very important to the rural people. (See Chapter 7 for more information.)

CHAPTER

10

FESTIVALS, HOLIDAYS, AND RECREATION

IN THE countryside, away from the influence of the larger cities, there is no such thing as a five or six day work week. The peasants toil day in and day out, from dawn to dark, until the work is completed. Relief only comes with the advent of a national holiday or a special festival.

The holidays and festivals are generally based on the lunar calendar. For this reason, their festivals may come on a different date each year by our Gregorian calendar.

The Lunar Calendar As with the Chinese, the Vietnamese lunar calendar begins with the year 2637 B.C. It has 12 months of 29 or 30 days each, and the year totals 355 days.

At approximately every third year, an extra month is included between the third and fourth months. This is to reconcile the lunar calendar with the solar one.

The Vietnamese like the lunar calendar because they can be sure of a full moon on the 15th day of each month. In their everyday life, however, they use the Gregorian calendar.

Unlike our centuries of 100 years, the Vietnamese calendar is divided into 60-year periods called "Hoi."

This "Hoi" or 60-year period is divided into two shorter cycles; one of a ten-year cycle and the other of a 12-year cycle.

The ten-year cycle, called "Can" is composed of ten heavenly stems. Their names and approximate translation follow.

1. Giap water in nature
2. At water in the home
3. Binh lighted fire
4. Dinh latent fire
5. Mau wood of all types
6. Ky wood set to burn
7. Canh metal of all kinds
8. Tan wrought metal
9. Nham virgin land
10. Quy cultivated land

The 12-year cycle, "Ky," has 12 earthy stems represented by the names of 12 names in the zodiac. Their names and translations in order are:

1. Ty the rat
2. Suu the buffalo
3. Dan the tiger
4. Meo the cat
5. Thin the dragon
6. Ty the snake

7. Ngo the horse
8. Mui the goat
9. Than the monkey
10. Dau the cock (the chicken)
11. Tuat the dog
12. Hoi the pig

A Vietnamese year is named after the combination of one of the names of the ten heavenly stems and one of the names of the 12 earthly stems. For instance, 1964 was the Year of the Dragon, "Giap-Thin." Giap is the first of the ten-year cycles and Thin is the fifth of the 12-year cycle. The year 1965 was "At-Ty." This follows down the line each year. The ten-year stem is not usually mentioned when discussing the year. Thus, we hear, "The Year of the Dragon" or the "Year of the Snake," etc., Giap-Thin, the Year of the Dragon, will not return for a 60-year period. This is true of all combinations.

The Dragon The Dragon is often spoken of or seen in replica in celebrations and festivals in Vietnam. The Vietnamese think he is a fabulous animal and represent him in Sino-Vietnamese mythology in the following manner.

He has the head of a camel, horns of a buck, eyes of a demon (bulging from their sockets), ears of a buffalo, neck and body of a snake, scales of a carp, claws of an eagle and paws of a tiger.

A long barbel hangs down at each side of the dragon's mouth, and a precious stone can be seen under his bright tongue. He will have a bony knot sticking out on the top of his head. In Vietnam, this is considered to be a mark of superior intelligence. The final characteristic of the dragon is that he will have 81 scaly points running along his backbone.

The dragon breathes out a vapour which he can change to fire or water at any time. He is considered to be immortal and does not reproduce himself. His habitat can be the air, in the water or under the ground.

The way the number of dragons multiplies is with the physical transformation of a half-lizard, half-snake reptile called the "Giao Long." When the "Giao Long" becomes, 1,000 years old, a sack under his throat disappears, and he is transformed into a dragon.

Even though the dragon is a frightening looking animal, he is not considered an evil spirit in Vietnam. In fact, both in China and in Vietnam, the dragon is an emblem of power and nobility.

HOLIDAYS AND FESTIVALS BY THE LUNAR CALENDAR

(Items with an asterisk will be discussed in detail. Many religious holidays are not included in this list)

LUNAR CALENDAR	HOLIDAY	ADDITIONAL INFORMATION
1st day 1st month	Le Van Duyet Day	Chapter 2
1st–7th day 1st month	Tet—New Year's*	Chapter 12
6th day 2nd month	Hai-Ba-Trung Day*	Chapter 2
5th day 3rd month	Thanh Mihh—Holiday of the Dead*	

LUNAR CALENDAR	HOLIDAY	ADDITIONAL INFORMATION
8th day 4th month	Celebration of Birth, Enlightenment and Death of Buddha	Chapter 4
17th day 4th month	Hung-Vuong Day	Chapter 2
5th day 5th month	Doan-Ngu—Summer Solstice Ceremony*	
15th day 6th month	Whale Festival*	
15th day 7th month	Trung Nguyen—Wandering Souls' Day*	
15th day 8th month	Trung Thu—Mid-Autumn Festival, Children's Holiday*	
20th day 8th month	Tran-Hung-Dao Day	Chapter 2
22nd day 8th month	Le-Loi Day	Chapter 2
28th day 9th month	Confucius' Birthday	Chapter 4

Tet (Nguyen Dan) New Year's Tet is the big event of the year in Vietnam, corresponding with the American's Christmas, New Year, Easter, and Fourth of July combined. It marks the beginning of the lunar New Year and Spring simultaneously. The holiday usually falls in late January or early February.

Tet is a time when everyone wants to be at his own home, which should be sparkling clean and full of flowers. New clothing is desired for everyone and presents are given.

For months before the new year, businessmen are getting ready for the big selling season. It is very difficult for foreigners to get tailoring work done in Vietnam right before Tet, as the tailors are very busy working for the local population. The items which are the greatest in demand are clothing, food, candles, and flowers. Practically every family forgets thrift and buys a large quantity of food for the Tet holidays, not only to eat but to place on the altar for the ancestors. Downtown streets are a riot of color with flowers and decorations at each store, including temporary ones, set up on the sidewalk.

All Vietnamese want to pay off their debts, as it is bad luck to owe money during Tet. Employers give their employees bonuses at this time of year and it is also a time that petty thefts increase. The items stolen are sold in order to have enough money for the holidays.

In addition, Tet is a time for correcting all faults, forgetting past mistakes, pardoning others for their offenses and no longer having enemies. One should behave in a friendly manner to all and should not have any grudges, envy or malice at this time. Even the Viet-Cong call an annual truce during Tet.

All of the busy activities of preparing for Tet come to an abrupt end at noon preceeding the beginning of the holiday. Merchants reduce their prices, sell everything they can, and shut their doors. Servants are let off work and everyone heads for home. If a person can possibly get home, no matter how far, he goes. The sidewalks are practically "rolled-up" and hardly any business is transacted during the holidays.

Home Activites On the afternoon before Tet of "Tat Nien" (New Year ceremony) a special ceremony takes place at which a sacrifice is offered to the deceased relatives and they are invited to come back for a few days and share the festivities with the living members of the family.

At midnight on New Year's Eve, a ceremony called "Giao Thua" is held in which a sacrifice for the spirits and the ancestors is made on a lovely candle-lit altar in the open air near the home. Fire-crackers which heralded in the new year may still be heard. (See Chapter 12.) After this, the family may break off some new buds from the special new plants and trees recently purchased for Tet and go to the Pagoda. There, they place incense before the altar and pray for the prosperity of the new year. When they leave the pagoda, another new bud is picked from a plant or tree and placed on the top of a column at their home on returning. This symbolizes good luck.

The next morning, the family arises early and dress in their new clothes. Dishes of special foods are prepared to be placed on the family altar for the ancestors who are back in the home during Tet. This will be repeated twice daily until Tet is over.

Everyone offers each other New Year wishes, and the children are given lucky red envelopes containing money. Tradition attaches great importance to the first visitor from outside the home on the New Year. He is believed to influence the happiness or well-being of the family during the rest of the year. If a rich man visits first, the family's fortune will increase. A man with a good name such as Phuoc which means "happiness" is preferable to one named Cho, "dog." Some families do not trust anything to luck. They invite their first guests and discourage those they consider unlucky not to come early. Generally, the visitors receive some form of refreshment at each home they visit.

On the fourth day of Tet, the Vietnamese believe that their ancestors return to their heavenly abode. The stores begin to re-open and life regains its normalcy. People visit graves on this day acting as an escort for their departing ancestors.

On the seventh day of Tet, the "Cay Neu" is removed from in front of the home. It is a high bamboo pole that is set up on the last day of the old lunar year. Various items are placed on the top, including red paper with an inscription written on it; a small basket containing betel and areca nuts; wind chimes; and a small square of woven bamboo representing a barrier to stop the evil spirits. A few colorful cock feathers may also decorate the pole. The offerings in the basket are intended for the good spirits.

The Vietnamese believe that the good spirits of the household must report to heaven during Tet, so they take many precautionary measures to scare off the bad spirits who know the good ones are away. They do not rely completely on the Cay Neu because legend tells them that it cannot stop a certain bad spirit. It is necessary for lime powder to be scattered around the house and to draw, with lime also, a bow and an arrow in front of the threshold. More information on this and other legends regarding Tet are included in Chapter 12.

Things not to do at Tet Some things are considered to be very bad luck if done at Tet. A few of them are as follows. Never clean house during Tet. Do not insult others or misbehave. Do not use profanity. Do not look fretful or show any anger or grief. Do not break any dishes. Make sure that you do not go in the wrong direction according to the lunar calendar.

There are also many other negative commandments and superstitions about Tet.

Hai-Ba-Trung Day This has been a special day for women in South Vietnam and celebrates the anniversary of the death of the Trung Sisters. The two sisters led a revolt against the ruling Chinese and won freedom for Vietnam in A.D. 41.

The driving force for their leadership was provided when one of the sister's husband was killed by the Chinese and in retaliation she successfully formed the revolutionary army which defeated the Chinese.

The sisters made Me-Ling in North Vietnam the capital of the freed country. Their reign was short-lived, however, only three years. The Chinese recaptured Vietnam and the sisters, in deep sorrow, drowned themselves in the Hat-Ciang River.

An interesting monument stood at the foot of Hai-Ba-Trung Street in Saigon on the waterfront commemorating the two sisters. Many people said the face on one of the sisters was that of Madame Nhu, the disliked sister-in-law of President Ngo Dinh Diem. According to a Vietnamese writer, on this holiday Madame Nhu once rode in a parade atop an elephant, as one of the Trung sisters. On the successful coup d'etat of November 1, 1963, a jubilant mob tore the statue apart. They did this because of their dislike for Madam Nhu, not because of the Trung sister's history.

Thanh Minh Holiday of the Dead Thanh Minh Day might be compared with the American Memorial Day. Families of deceased persons prepare offerings consisting of food, flowers, incense sticks, votive papers, etc., and pay a visit to the grave. A few days before the visit, family members clean the area surrounding the grave, paint the tombs and make preparation for the solemn visit on the special holiday.

Doan Ngu This is a ceremony opening the summer solstice. Vietnam is a tropical country and during the summer solstice, it seems that the worst fate awaits its inhabitants. Epidemics of plague, cholera, flu, etc. often occur during this season. Most Vietnamese people believe that these illnesses are brought on by harmful spirits. They think that the God of Death is especially severe during this time of year because he needs souls for his army in hell. Because of this, he causes epidemics in order to get more soldiers.

During this celebration, people also pray for coolness. Altars are erected in pagodas, temples or at public places for the celebration throughout the country. People make offerings to spirits, ghosts, and the god of death. They burn votive papers, and effigies of human beings are burned in an effort to satisfy the god of death with the soldiers he needs. The ceremonies are led by Buddhist monks. In addition, many families place an amulet at their door as an added protection against epidemics.

The Whale Festival This festival is not typical of the whole country since it is held in only one locality. However, it is typical of the many different festivals held in villages in Vietnam. Different groups often have their own festivals.

Vam-Lang, a village south of Saigon, is the scene of the interesting Whale Festival. A three day festival, the highlight is at midnight on the first day.

A motorboat, illuminated with pretty colored lamps, carrying an altar which symbolizes the whale, and full of musicians playing traditional Vietnamese music, heads out to sea. After a short time, the boat returns to the village and the altar is carried to the temple with cymbals and tomtoms playing wildly. The symbolic altar is placed on another altar "of the whale" in the incense-filled temple. Beside the altar, there are several small coffins which hold the remains of whales that died at sea and were brought back by fishermen. The whale, which is considered to be the benefactor of all fishermen, is thought to remain, in spirit, with all of those present at the celebration.

Trung Nguyen (Wandering Souls' Day) This is the second largest festival of the year. (Tet is first.) Though it falls on the 15th day of the seventh month, its celebration may be held at any convenient time during the latter half of the month. The festival is celebrated throughout the country, in Buddhist Pagodas, homes, businesses, factories, government offices, and Armed Forces units. It is not just a Buddhist holiday, but one celebrated by all Vietnamese who believe in the existence of God, good and evil.

Many Vietnamese believe that every person has two souls; one is spiritual (Hon), and the other is material (Via). When a person dies, his soul is taken to a tribunal in hell and judged by ten justices. When judgment is rendered, the soul is sent to heaven or hell, as a reward or punishment for the person's conduct on earth.

They believe that sinful souls can be absolved of their punishment and delivered from hell through prayers said by the living on the first and 15 of every month. Wandering Souls' Day however, is believed to be the best time for priests and relatives to secure general amnesty for all the souls. On this day, the gates of hell are said to be opened at sunset and the souls there fly out, unclothed and hungry. Those who have relatives fly back to their homes and villages and find plenty of food on their family altars.

Those who have no relatives or have been forsaken by the living, are doomed to wander helplessly through the air on black clouds, over the rivers and from tree to tree. They are the sad "wandering souls" who are in need of food and prayer. This is why additional altars full of offerings are placed in pagodas and many public places.

This is a day that the oldsters have said, "the living and the dead meet in thought," and traditional rites should be respected by all. Weather permitting, the services should be in the open air. Otherwise, the largest room in the house should be used so that there is room for many wandering souls.

During the ceremony, huge tables are covered with offerings which basically consist of three kinds of meat: boiled chicken, roast pork, and crabs; and five fruits. Other foods may be included such as sticky rice cakes, vermicelli soup, and meat rolls to satisfy the appetite of the wandering souls who are supposed to be hungry the year round.

Money and clothes made of votive papers are also burned at this time.

Butcher shops are especially careful to observe this holiday, because many people believe in reincarnation and butchers are afraid that they might have killed some poor person. (See Chapter 4 for more on this belief.)

Also, Vietnamese believe it is extremely bad luck to die away from home, so transportation carriers who have had fatalities among its passengers strictly observe the ceremonies.

Trung Thu Mid-Autumn Festival

This is a delightful festival for children and most pleasant for the adults to watch. Many weeks before the festival, bakers are busy making hundreds of thousands of moon cakes of sticky rice and filled with all kinds of unusual fillings such as peanuts, sugar, lotus seed, duck-egg yolks, raisins, watermelon seed, etc. They are baked and sold in colorful boxes. Expensive ones in ornate boxes are presented as gifts.

Also made in advance are colorful lanterns made in the form of boats, dragons, hares, toads, lobsters, unicorns, carp, etc. These are sold for weeks on the streets of every village and city. The children begin playing with them long before the holiday. They light little candles and place them inside the lanterns made of cellophane paper and swing them around on sticks, all in the darkness of the evening. It is one of the most beautiful sights to see in Vietnam during the year.

On the night of the festival, children form a procession and go through the streets holding their lighted lanterns and performing the dances of the unicorn to the accompaniment of drums and cymbals.

There are many legendary origins of the festival, but the one most accepted in Vietnam is that it began during the reign of Emperor Minh-Hoang of the Duong Dynasty. Legend says that he took his empress, Duong-Quy-Pho, to a lake called Thai Dick on the 15th day of the 8th lunar month where they admired the moon. When the moon was at its brightest, the emperor composed a poem and explained it to his wife. He loved to read the verses in the moonlight.

Moon cakes were supposedly used at other times in Chinese history. Secret messages were placed inside the cakes to inform the people of a revolt to be held against a hated ruler during one of the many internal wars in China.

RECREATION

GAMBLING has played an important role in the social and recreational habits of the Vietnamese. Children may be seen tossing coins, stones, or sticks along the streets playing different games. Gambling is included in many of them.

The national lottery is well-liked in South Vietnam and provides beneficial side results. Money derived from the sale of lottery tickets goes into reconstruction and industrial development funds in the national treasury. In addition, thousands of people are given some means of making a living by selling tickets. They receive a commission and often tips. Every Vietnamese seems to have a dream of winning a million piastres some day in the weekly drawings. There have been a few cases of corruption in the history of the national lottery.

Card playing and mahjong are especially popular with adults. Another favorite pastime with children and adults alike is betting on cricket fights during the rainy season. Children catch crickets and sell them for this purpose.

Horse racing held on Saturday and Sunday in a Saigon suburb draws large crowds as thousands of Vietnamese, young and old, turn out to cheer the pint-sized Asiatic horses and jockeys on to victory. Betting is heavy, with profits going into the national treasury of South Vietnam. It is not uncommon to see a horse run the wrong way around the track.

Other popular sporting events include soccer, basketball, volleyball, swimming, hiking, ping pong, and tennis. Vietnam teams often compete with other countries in soccer, tennis, bicycling, basketball, and other sports.

There are few golf courses in South Vietnam. The one in Saigon is located near Tan Son Nhut Airport. It may well be the only golf course in the world fortified by pillbox installations on its perimeter, with soldiers and machine guns inside. There is an excellent golf course in Dalat. Caddies are usually women.

There is hardly any television in Vietnam, and the people are avid movie and theater-goers. Films from all over the world are shown in theaters throughout the country.

Another favorite teen-age and adult pasttime is "bird watching"—meaning people watching. They love to sit in cafes facing the street with doors wide open allowing a good view of the street and watch the world go by.

For those who can afford it, restaurants and night clubs are popular. They especially like to go to those places offering rotating vocalists who go from one entertainment establishment to another on a schedule. A person may stay in one place all evening and hear a dozen or so different entertainers.

Country people often think up their own amusements. They are very resourceful and use whatever is available. Those along the sea-shore may have boat races with the small round bamboo boats that look as if they could tip over at any moment. In the areas where elephants are found, they may be raced in competition with each other.

Children amuse themselves very well in Vietnam. Even though they seldom have fancy toys, they always seem to be able to find something to interest them. Due to the large number of children living in small areas, this is not hard to do.

CHAPTER 11

PLACES OF INTEREST

VIETNAM has many attractions which would please even the most seasoned world travelers. Unfortunately, it has often been over-looked as a place to visit because of the unsettling wars that have gone on in the country. Still, there is much that can and should be seen.

Due to the changing circumstances, it is advisable to check with your Embassy before embarking on visits outside of the major cities.

The sights to see range from modern, late-day developments to relics from the earliest civilizations. The countryside also varies with a change in scenery available by traveling a few extra miles.

With the new jet services to Saigon, it is possible to go from San Francisco to Saigon via the Pacific in about 18 hours. Travel time from Washington via the European route is about 27 hours. It cost a little over $100 more to take the longer route.

Air connections are available from Hong Kong, the Philippines, Japan, and Thailand. Bangkok is a good transfer point with over 20 major air-lines connecting with Saigon. Sea transportation by well-known shipping lines is also available.

Travel to North Vietnam for U.S. citizens is prohibited by the American government.

Within the country, the only safe means of transportation between cities is by air. A jet service is now in operation between Saigon, Da-Nang, and Hue, and piston aircraft have regular runs to the larger Vietnamese cities including Dalat, Nha-Trang, Qui-Nhon, Da-Nang, Hue, Banmethuout, Pleiku, Kontum, Tuy-Hoa, and Quang-Ngai. Flights to other cities may be chartered on smaller planes. Air Vietnam is the national airline. It holds a good safety record and has experienced and well-trained pilots. A large number of French pilots are employed and usually fly the larger aircraft.

Saigon-Cholon Saigon is the capital of South Vietnam. It is a city that makes one think of Paris, with its tree-lined streets and smart shops. There is nothing quite so invigorating as to take a cyclo (a comfortable chair on wheels powered by a man pedalling a bicycle) early in the morning before the city gets hot, and ride through the streets of Saigon watching the people and their children get to the business at hand for the day.

Tu-Do Street is noted for its fine shops and a variety of hotels. There are still a couple of open-air restaurants on this street where the more daring sip their French coffee, wines, or Vietnamese beer, acting unconcerned about the hand grenade that may be tossed in at any given moment. Formerly, there were many sidewalk cafes with their colorful umbrellas unfurled along Saigon's streets, but these had to be closed because of Viet-Cong terrorism.

Most of the public buildings in this area were constructed in the years around 1900 and are in the old French style. They contrast nicely with the new strong-lined modern buildings, giving the city a charm all of its own.

Many pagodas are well worth a visit, including the now famous Xa-Loi Buddhist Pagoda, which served as the headquarters of the Buddhist led revolt against the Diem regime. There is also an Indian temple, Chettys, off Tu-Do street. An interesting Chinese pagoda is Quai de Belgique.

The Botanical Gardens and the zoo which are located near each other will keep one interested for visit after visit and are very popular with the Vietnamese. The garden has one of the best collections of orchids and equatorial plants in the world. The zoo is outstanding and one of the most spacious and well-kept in Asia. This is a place to hold on to your wallet, as many of the charming children huddle around you and often earn their money by picking pockets. Many of them are homeless. Here the signs could read, "please do feed the animals," as sugar-cane is sold for the elephants and peanuts and other goodies for other animals.

The National Museum, built with the help of the French School of the Extreme Orient, contains a unique collection of relics of every phase of the history of civilization in the Indo-China peninsula.

A whole book could be written on the fantastic city of Saigon, and one leaves it with a sense of regret at not having seen or absorbed enough of what it has to offer. More information on unusual things to see are included in the latter part of this chapter.

Cholon is a sister city of Saigon and the two are joined by a two mile four-lane boulevard full of taxis, cars, bicycles, motor bikes, cyclos, carts, and every other known vehicle.

The best time to go to Cholon is at night when the bright lights of Chinatown beckon you to the many gastronomical wonders inside. The city is often thought to be just a little more "wicked" than Saigon and has had the reputation of housing gambling establishments and other places of dubious entertainment. Some of the better night clubs are located in this area.

The majority of Vietnam's Chinese population lives in this area. It has been almost traditional that the Chinese segregate themselves in Vietnam.

The best way to see Cholon is to hire a cyclo for a number of hours, ride through the streets and stop at will. Be sure to settle the price of the cyclo in advance. Cholon is a charming place to spend an afternoon and evening. There are a few schools in this area which have had mostly American teachers for the pupils, so do not be surprised if a friendly "Hi!" comes from one of the youngsters you run into. Having taught in this city, I can assure you that you will probably never meet a more hospitable people. For that matter, the same thing applies to most Vietnamese.

Gia-Dinh There are two particular things of interest to see in this suburb of Saigon which may be reached by taxi. One is the tomb of Marshal Le Van Duyet, who served under the Emperor Gia-Long. The burial place was destroyed under the direction of the Emperor Minh Mang in 1831. He also had the coffin symbolically lashed because of his displeasure with Le Van Duyet. Gia-Long, Minh Mang's father, had asked Le Van Duyet to help his son and advise him, but Minh Mang only hated Le Van Duyet all the more. The tomb was rebuilt by Thieu Tri, Minh Mang's successor.

Also in Gia-Dinh is the tomb of the Bishop of Adran of France. The tomb bears an inscription telling of the friendship between the French prelate and the Emperor Gia Long.

Bien-Hoa Bien-Hoa may be reached by a modern four-lane highway built under the American Aid program. It is about 20 miles from Saigon and is located on the banks of the Dong-Nai River, bordering the famous hunting regions of Cum Tien plateau and the Lagna plain.

The interesting things to see in Bien-Hoa are the Buu-Son Temple and the Art School. Located in the Buu-Son Temple is a 15th century granite statue of Cham origin. It was hidden for several centuries in a tree trunk. The Art School is one of the most important in Vietnam, and many fascinating pieces of sculpture and ceramics can be purchased here at reasonable prices. It is most interesting to see the talented Vietnamese artists at work. They specialize in pottery and bronze.

Vung Tau (Cap St-Jacques) and Tri An Vung Tau, located approximately 77 miles from Saigon by road, is a popular seaside resort particularly liked by the French residents of South Vietnam. It is still frequented by hundreds of cool, calm, and collected Saigon residents on weekends even though the road they drive on is subject to Viet-Cong terrorism at any minute. The beach at Vung Tau is not nearly as beautiful as the one at Nha-Trang, but is far more accessible to the weekend holiday enthusiast. There are many Americans stationed there. The traveler arriving in Vietnam by sea will get a glimpse of this area as he comes into the Dong-Nai River and heads up the river to Saigon.

The Tri An waterfalls, a real sight to see in the rainy season, are also located in this area.

Dalat Located in the Central Highlands just 145 air miles from Saigon, Dalat can be described as the resting place for all of South Vietnam's local travelers. It is a delightfully cool area in the mountains and a welcome respite from the tropical heat that most of the country endures.

Dalat is a romantic, gracious, and stately town with an elevation of 4,920 feet above sea level. It is surrounded by pine woods and flowering gardens. The air is clean, fresh and very invigorating. There are lovely houses with beautiful lawns and gardens. Orchids are a specialty here. The beautiful lake was man-made for water sports and relaxation. Tennis courts and one of the best golf courses in Asia are located there.

Dalat is the home of the Vietnamese Military Academy, the Armed Forces Staff College, the Geographic Institute of Vietnam, and the University of Dalat, the only private university in South Vietnam. The Triga Nuclear Reactor is also in Dalat. It was placed in operation in 1963 under an Atoms for peace grant from the United States.

The Dalat Market, built with American Aid, is one of the

most modern in Asia. The choice fruits and vegetables grown in Dalat and shipped throughout the country are at their peak of perfection in this fine market.

The city also boasts a most unusual zoo. Animal cages and pits are situated in clearings in the woods, similar to the animals' natural habitats.

Dalat, by far, has a reputation as being the paradise for hunters in Vietnam. Within two hours, there is wonderful hunting land full of game, including stag, roe-deer, peacocks, pheasants, boar, black bear, ox, panthers, tigers, and elephants. It is best to have a professional hunter as a guide in Vietnam. During the Viet-Cong insurgency, it has been risky for Americans to hunt there as often they turn out to be the hunted. Several American servicemen have lost their lives on hunting trips in Vietnam—not to tigers, but to the Viet-Cong. When the conflict in Vietnam is settled, this area can be a playground for all of Asia.

Nha-Trang A beach that is praised most is the one in Nha-Trang. A range of mountains frame the beach and make one think of Hawaii. The bay encircles coral reefs, and the sand is a beautiful white. It is delightful to see the native children, swimming naked and running along the beaches, completely uninhibited by the cares of the modern world or the pains of war going on nearby. Boat trips are popular for a visit to the nearby islands, especially skin diving in the clear waters around them.

The Institute of Oceanography and Fisheries is located in Nha-Trang and studies the conditions for fishing along the coast and draws up catalogs for the many scientific processes dealing with fishing and fish by-products, such as fish flour, which plays an important role in the Vietnamese diet.

The Po-Nagar sanctuaries are located on a high hill near Nha-Trang. They were built during the earliest Cham civilization and date back to the 7th century. They are one of the few original buildings still standing in Vietnam despite the ravages of time, climate, and wars.

Da-Nang (Tourane) This city was once one of Vietnam's most beautiful, noted for its tasty lobster and crab. Today, it has lost some of its beauty and charm because it seems to be more a city at war than Saigon, 385 air miles to the south.

It is the site of America's largest air base in Vietnam and also is an important port which has been described as equalling the beauty of the Bay of Naples. The French School of the Extreme Orient has excavated at the nearby Cham towns of Mi Son and Tra Kieu and found a highly advanced culture in existence as far back as the 6th century, and believe the Khmer civilization sprang from here. There is a museum showing the relics uncovered by the French group. Marble Mountain, across the river from Da-Nang, offers interesting sightseeing and hand-made marble objects.

Hue Approximately 400 air miles north of Saigon, Hue is the former capital of the Annamite Empire. An aristocratic and elegant city, Hue is noted for its beautiful women. It is near the 17th parallel where the North and South of Vietnam are divided.

Hue is called the Imperial City and is a place where if one takes a little time it is possible to learn a great deal about

Vietnamese civilization. At Vau-Ban, the walls of the former mighty citadel, over two and one half miles long, surround the place where the emperor and his entourage lived. One enters it through huge bastioned doors on the banks of the Perfume River.

The Imperial tombs are located close to Hue. Here are two artificially-built hills which were built to defend the city against evil spirits and also an ancient Cham pyramid. It has been said that these tombs are far more magnificant than the renowned counterparts in China. The six most famous tombs are those of the Emperor Gia-Long, Minh-Mang, Thieu-Tri, Tu-Duc, Dong-Khanh, and Khai-Dinh.

The second largest university in South Vietnam is also located in Hue.

Ban-Me-Thuot An area that is representative of the mountaineer kingdom and its people is Ban-Me-Thuot. It is located about 165 air miles north of Saigon. The people of the highlands are quite different from those in the lowlands. They have been ignored by many, discriminated against by most and have grown to be the "special children" of the American Special Forces and American Aid personnel. American missionaries have also taken an intense interest in these people, formulating written languages for them and ministering to their physical and spiritual needs. More information may be found in Chapter 3.

In the event that it is impractical to travel to this area, examples of the mountain people can be found near Dalat. It should be recognized, however, that the mountaineers around Dalat are far more used to the outside world than those of the remote areas.

NORTH VIETNAM

As I HAVE not visited any cities in North Vietnam, my accounts of that area will be information gathered from published books and pamphlets and from interviews with friends with the International Control Commission who have visited North Vietnam on official business.

Hanoi Hanoi is a beautiful city situated on the Red River about 60 miles from the port of Haiphong. It served as the capital of the Annamite Empire until the 18th century.

A beautiful lake marks the center of the city. It is surrounded by gardens and is a meeting place for weary people after a day's work.

Only a few traces remain of the old citadel which was built by the Emperor Gia-Long between 1805 and 1812. It was destroyed in 1892. The Mirado, the Royal Pagoda, the North Gate, and other old ramparts still stand.

There are still many pagodas dated from the 8th to the 10th centuries hidden away in the city. Some of the most famous are the Island of Jade, Van Mieu, the One Column Pagoda, the Temple of the Dark Warrior, and the Pagoda of the Grand Buddha.

Several small villages, famous for making paper and pottery, are located near Hanoi.

Haiphong Haiphong is an inland port located 25 miles from the Gulf of Tonkin. It is one of the principal industrial and commercial cities of the north and is important as a transit port. The city was built in 1874. A lot of public works have been undertaken there, such as the draining of marshes, building of wharves, etc. The industrial development has grown, mainly because of the closeness of coal mines and also because the Hanoi railroad which is extended to the Chinese province of Yunnan, has its terminus at Haiphong.

The Bay of Ha-Long (Along)

A great deal has been written in Vietnam about the Bay of Ha-Long. Considered one of the world's unique marvels, it is a huge "sea" studded with thousands of islets and isles covering an area of approximately 1,000 square miles.

If you can imagine a vast mountainous area with cliffs and crests which suddenly fell down into the sea leaving just the summits of the mountains protruding above the level of the sea, and eroded by the slow work of waves, then you can have a fairly accurate picture of the bay. There are large islands with ruffled beaches, surfs against steep cliffs, crags sticking up like pyramids, towers, pillars, monumental arches, and giant porticoes, all mixed together in a stretch of more than 60 miles. Some are named, such as the Toad, the Sail, and the Unicor. A few of the most fascinating sites include the Grotto of Wonders, Grotto of Surprise, the Circus of Surprise, the Three Circuses, and the Tunnel of the Customs House.

From an industrial point of view, the most interesting might be the coal mines of Hongay. The huge steps going up the sides of a mountain to the mine can be seen from a boat in the bay. There are numerous open-air coal mines, considered to be among the most important in that area of the world. Looking from a boat, it is said that the 10,000 or so workers look like ants, boring, hewing, and cutting the gigantic blocks. The coal is thrown into carts which are transported on an inclined plane, and a network of railways, to two artificial deepwater harbours, Hongay and Campha-Port.

According to experts, in the geological eras a stupendous earthquake occurred in North Vietnam which caused the upheaval of rocky masses of calcareous formation. These are found in the Bay of Ha-Long as well as inland in the Lang-Son and Cao-Bang regions and the Red River delta. There, they look like continuous walls or big lonely peaks along the fertile plain, where they have gradually been embedded by the deposits left by the Red River during thousands of years.

The Bay of Ha-Long means "Dragon's Den" in the native language. It is said to be named after a huge sea monster of such dimensions that it causes a change of tide when entering or leaving its den.

The Higher Regions There is an especially picturesque road which runs through the main tourist centers of the higher regions along the Chinese border. It goes through such mountain towns as Lang-Son and Cao-Bank, which are surrounded by pretty suburban villages. In one area, where the road stops at Cho-Ba, there are a series of lakes called the Ba-Be lakes. They are five miles long and are overlooked by steep mountains ranging between 2,000 and 6,000 feet in altitude.

Mountain Resorts There are two mountain resorts, Tam-Dao and Cha-Pa which attract people from the cities during heat waves.

Tam-Dao is 40 miles from Hanoi and is 3,000 feet above sea-level, and overlooks the plain of the Red River delta.

Cha-Pa, located just 20 miles from Hanoi, is supposed to be the most delightful resort in all North Vietnam. It is located at 5,000 feet above sea-level and overhung by a 7,000-foot mountain peak. The resort is located admidst the highest mountains of Indochina.

OFF THE BEATEN PATH

THERE ARE many unusual things to see and do that may never be found listed in the guide-books. Experience is the best teacher. Included here are a few places and experiences that our family enjoyed most in Vietnam.

Saigon Animal and Bird Market An extremely interesting place to spend a few hours in the morning is at the Pet Market near the American Embassy on Ham Nghi street. Vendors sell the pets right on the side-walk, and an amazing variety of animals and birds are sold. Even deer may be found there. Occasionally when one loses a pet in Saigon, the owner searches the market, as the pet may well turn up for sale.

Saigon's Wall Street Also located on Ham Nghi Street near the American Embassy is an area known as Saigon's "Wall Street." The busiest places are located near the French National Bank and the Bangkok Bank just behind the National Bank of Vietnam.

Here, businessmen from all walks of life gather early in the morning at the cafes and in small groups on the sidewalks to make deals and observe market prices and exchange rates. The businessmen hustle about from one place to the other, and timing is important if they are to settle a deal at just the right moment. Many of them are paid agents. This is reminiscent of the early days of the U.S. Wall Street trading methods.

One may spend a full morning watching the business dealings of a country being transacted over a cup of coffee or a glass of beer, right under your nose. There is no official stock exchange in Vietnam.

Saigon's Flower Street Nguyen-Hue, Saigon's Flower Street, is fun to walk down at any given hour, but it is really in its glory during the Vietnamese New Year, Tet celebration. Sometimes the whole street is closed off and flower venders take over completely, selling the plants, shrubs, and flowers that are a must in every Vietnamese home during Tet. Shutterbugs should make a special effort to be in Saigon during this time.

DINING OUT

THERE ARE many good restaurants, but after two years' experience in Saigon, three favorites emerge for excellent food and reasonable prices.

MAYFAIR—40 B, Gia-Long. Quiet atmosphere, excellent service, great soups, and steaks.

MY CANH—Floating Restaurant on Saigon River.

This restaurant was recently the scene of a Viet-Cong bombing. It was soon back in operation, true to form in Vietnam. It has been a pleasant place to forget the day's troubles and cool off right after sunset, watching the boats and people go by.

Excellent Chinese food.

INTERNATIONAL—91 Cong Ly

Good Chinese food and a representative evening of Vietnamese entertainment as the loveliest singers in Vietnam sing for about fifteen minutes each. When they leave, they rotate to other restaurants and clubs.

Excellent French and Chinese menu.

OTHER ENTERTAINMENT

NHA-TRANG—Cyclo races

Great fun at night. Hire your cyclo and agree on the price in advance. Have your friends do the same. Fastest cyclo driver gets a bonus at the end of the long four-lane beach road. Most people race from one beach bar to the next, which are numbered from 1 to 14 instead of named. Some Americans like to put the driver in the seat and drive the cyclos themselves!

FRANCOIS'S

A place not to miss in Nha-Trang is Francois's. It is a mangy-looking place located down by the boat landings at the village of Cau-Da. On first glance, it looks as if the Board of Health should close it, but food like this is not to be found elsewhere, especially the lobster. Francois picks them out himself and is known to stock only the best. Actually, they are really crayfish in this area. They are huge, meaty, and tender, never stringy. The "natives" joke that the Americans should leave by ten because the Viet-Cong come in to eat *their* lobster then.

VUNG-TAU

Go to see Irene, the owner of Irene's bar. She is the "girl next door" personified. A real beauty of Greek and Vietnamese heritage, Irene has supported her whole family including her disabled father and mother and their ten children, by running a bar.

The unusual thing about Irene is that she is a legend in those parts with the Americans. Despite her occupation and her beauty, she is a very nice girl whom the American men have protected like a sister.

THU-DAU-MOT—near Saigon

See the lacquer craftsmen at work creating objects of beauty in its many painstaking stages. See the manager at Thanh-Le on Tu Do Street for further information.

TAY-NINH—about 60 miles NW of Saigon

Try to see the ceremonies at the Cao-Dai temple. This is a very fascinating religion which had the French writer Victor Hugo as one of its patrons.

Hue A ride down the Perfume River with a couple of musicians on your boat and dinner served from *hibachis* is an evening to be remembered. Be sure and check on security, or it might end up as a venture you would like to forget!

CHAPTER 12

LEGENDS OF VIETNAM

THE VIETNAMESE people love to hear stories of long ago. It is a common sight to see little children sitting with their grandparents listening with awe to tales passed down through countless generations.

Many of the customs in use were brought about through legend. Tet time, or the lunar New Year, is a period that is especially influenced by customs.

Spreading of Lime Powder Around the House at Tet

Each year at Tet, Vietnamese spread lime powder around their home and draw a bow and arrow in the lime powder in front of their door.

Legend tells us that after defeating all the feudal lords and pacifying Vietnam, the Emperor Dinh-Tien-Hoang had to face an even more terrible enemy. Plague was spreading through the country. The emperor realized that there was nothing his army could do about this menace.

He asked for help from heaven and a *genii* appeared who ordered him to have lime spread around every home in the kingdom of Vietnam. The *genii* also prescribed that a bow and arrow be drawn in front of each threshold to drive off the evil spirits. This was done and the plague subsided. The custom was thereby established and has remained until this day.

The Legend of the Apricot Tree

Apricot trees are very important at Tet also. Though the branches are now used mostly as an ornament, they were originally used to scare off evil spirits.

Once upon a time, there was a huge apricot tree, larger than all the others. The shade from its leaves covered a wide area of the ground below. Two *genii,* Tra and Uat Luy had chosen it as their home and mercilessly exterminated all the demons and phantoms in the entire area. Because of this, people living in this area were protected from the demons.

When the end of the lunar year came, Tra and Uat Luy, like all other divinities, had to go and offer their respects and good wishes to the Emperor of Jade. They left their home for a few days to do this, leaving the people living nearby at the mercy of the evil spirits. The people knew that the spirits were deathly afraid of the big apricot tree where the *genii* lived, so they each went and picked a branch from the tree and placed it on their door to scare the bad spirits away.

The Legend of the Narcissus

Like the apricot blossom, the narcissus plays an important role at Tet. It is considered a good omen if they bloom on New Year's Day, so great care is given to their cultivation, with the use of sugar water, gruning, and other techniques, to ensure their blooming at that time.

A rich old man had three sons. When he felt he was about to die, he called in his children and said that he wished his fortune to be divided equally among them. The children promised to respect his will and the old man died happy.

He had hardly been buried when the two elder sons took most of the youngest one's share. Only a poor plot of good-for-nothing-land was given to him.

The unfortunate younger son was sadly looking at his inheritance when he saw a fairy appear. "Stop crying," she said. "There is a treasure hidden beneath your plot of land and your brothers don't know it." She explained that the sprout of a most valuable flower was hidden under the soil.

The boy was astonished and the fairy said, "You'll get rich with these flowers; each spring will see them bloom in your garden and you can sell them at a good price."

The boy was filled with gratitude and prostrated himself on the ground to express his thanks, but the fairy had disappeared.

The very next spring, the land was covered with a fragrant whiteness. In memory of the fairy who protected him, he called the flower Thuy Tien (water fairy). Everyone who saw it loved its beauty and delicate perfume. The lords and the rich began to contend with one another to buy them and offered fabulous prices for the floral wonder.

In just a few years, the lucky fellow accumulated an immense fortune from the sale of the narcissus. As he became richer than his stingy brothers who tried to rob him, the narcissus became the symbol of success and prosperity. This is why it is used at Tet.

The Legend of Firecrackers

Tet could not be celebrated properly without firecrackers. They sound off like machine-guns at midnight before the New Year, blasting out the old and bringing in the new.

In ancient times, there were two wicked spirits who hated mankind and played many wicked tricks on the people. Their names were Na Ong and Na Ba, husband and wife. Both of them feared light and noise, however, so they did all their nasty deeds at night.

At Tet when the good *genii* of that neighborhood had to report to heaven, the two bad spirits were particularly bad and threw the people into a frenzy. The people learned that Na Ong and Na Ba were afraid of light and noise so they lighted their homes and exploded firecrackers to scare the bad *genii* away. They kept the noise and lights going strong until Tet was over and their good protectors could get back home from heaven. Then, the firecrackers and lights were no longer necessary.

The Betel and the Areca Tree

This legend explains why the betel nut is chewed by newlywed couples and at ceremonies and anniversaries.

During the reign of Hung-Vuong III, there was a mandarin by the name of Cao. He had two good-looking sons who resembled each other so much that many people thought they were twins. The two boys, Tan and Lang, were most fond of each other.

Tan and Lang's father and mother died, leaving them without any money. After a series of misfortunes, the boys decided they would try to find work. Guided by fate, the first place they went to was the home of a good friend of their father, Magistrate Luu. Luu welcomed the boys cordially and offered them a place in his stately mansion.

Luu accepted the boys as his own sons for he had never had a son, and this is considered to be a terrible fate in Vietnam. He did have a beautiful daughter, however, who was "as fair as a white lotus and as fresh as a spring rose." The magistrate wanted to tighten the bonds of affection and friendship between the boys and his family, so he decided to give his daughter in marriage to one of the boys.

Both of the boys were naturally attracted by the pretty maiden with her beautiful appearance and graceful manners and each of them loved her secretly. However, each of the boys had a generous heart and each one insisted that his beloved brother have the honor of marrying the Magistrate's lovely daughter.

The father knew the boys could never come to an agreement and because they looked like twins, he never had really known which brother was the eldest. He prepared a little trick to find out who was the elder brother, because he would offer his daughter to him. The eldest son in a family receives priority over the others, according to custom.

Luu ordered that a fine dinner be served to the brothers but told the servants that they were to put only one pair of chopsticks on the tables. The boys were seated and without hesitation, Lang picked up the chopsticks and respectfully handed them to Tan. Tan took them in a most natural manner as any elder brother would do. Therefore, Magistrate Luu chose Tan as the bridegroom.

Tan was now the happiest man in all of Vietnam. He loved his bride so passionately that he spent most of his time making up love poems to describe his feelings. He completely neglected his brother Lang, who seemed to have disappeared from his thoughts.

After the wedding of his brother to the fair maiden, Lang overcame his secret love for her and accepted his lot, for he wanted only joy and happiness for his beloved older brother.

After awhile, however, Lang realized that his brother was very cold and indifferent to him. Lang sat alone in his room waiting for some sign of care or friendship from his brother, but nothing happened.

Poor Lang! To him, this was the worst possible fate. His beloved brother no longer cared for him and he had also lost the love of his dreams. In wild sorrow, he ran away from his home, for he could stand the sadness no longer. He ran and ran, passing leafy forests, until he reached the dark blue sea. Night came and Lang fell exhausted on the ground, hungry and thirsty. His head was as hot as fire. He cried and cried until he died and was turned immediately into a white chalky rock.

Tan discovered that Lang had stolen away and he felt extremely sorry and ashamed for his selfishness toward the brother he loved. Full of regrets and worries, he set out to look for Lang.

He went along the same way that his brother had gone and arrived at the same dark blue sea. He, too, was exhausted and sat down by the white rock and began to weep. He wept and wept until he died and then he was turned into a tree with a straight stem and green palms. It was the areca tree.

The lovely maiden missed her husband, Tan, so much that she set off one day to look for him. She went along the same way as the brothers and reached the sea and lay down exhausted at the foot of the tall areca tree. Tears of despair rolled down her cheeks, and she cried sorrowfully until she died. She was turned into a creeping plant—the betel—which twined round the lofty column of the areca tree.

The peasants who lived near this place all had a dream about the three people and built a temple in commemoration of the fraternal and conjugal love of the three.

Years later, King Hung-Vuong III, happened to be in that place and he was puzzled by the rock, the tree, and the plant, all of which he had never seen before.

When he heard the whole story, he said, "If these are such devoted brothers and faithful husband and wife, let us mix up the three things together to see the result."

They burned the rock which became soft and white, and they wrapped a little of it in a betel leaf, cut a piece of areca nut and squeezed them all together. A sort of red liquid, like blood, ran out of the mixture.

The king thought a few minutes and said, "This is the true symbol of conjugal and fraternal love. Let the tree and the plant be grown everywhere in commemoration of this beautiful but sad story."

Brothers and sisters, and especially newlyweds, began to chew betel in order to maintain conjugal love. The habit spread very quickly and now a great number of people chew betel at all meetings to "maintain mutual affection."

(Adapted from a translation by Mrs. Bach Lan)

The Compassionate Protectress of Children

In some old Vietnamese pagodas, there is often found a statue of a woman carrying a child in her arms. She is the goddess Quan-Am-Tong-Tu (the compassionate protectress of children). The legend behind that story follows.

Once upon a time, there was a girl named Thi-Kinh, who came from a most humble family. She was industrious as well as beautiful and many men of means, including some of the most handsome men in that area, sought her hand in marriage. She refused them all and married a poor, simple man.

Life was hard for them from the beginning. They had just a few acres of rice-fields and they worked them alone. Despite all of the hard work, the young wife was undaunted and found great pleasure in giving love and devotion to her husband.

One summer afternoon, Thi-Kinh's husband was asleep in the hammock and the young wife whiled away the afternoon just gazing at his face. All at once, she noticed a hair of his beard, growing in the wrong direction on his chin. She took a sharp knife and approached her husband with the intention of shaving off that hair. She had just barely touched his face with the knife when he awoke with a start. Frightened, he began to scream, accusing his wife of trying to kill him.

Stunned by the terrible accusation and all of the neighbors who came running, she did not say a word to vindicate herself. Her husband and the neighbors took this silence as an admission of guilt. Thi-Kihn was cast out of her home and no one felt sorry for her.

Thi-Kinh felt lost because everyone had turned against her, even her own family. She decided to renounce the world and find forgetfullness.

Disguised as a man, she entered a religious order in an old pagoda. Despite the simplicity of the religious garments she wore and her head being shaved, Thi-Kinh was, indeed, handsome and the people frequenting the pagoda often commented on how handsome "he" was.

Before long, a pretty young girl fell in love with the handsome monk (Thi-Kinh in disguise) and tried in vain to get his attentions. In desperation, the young girl approached the monk one day and began to spill out her feelings for him. Before she could finish, her words were cut short and she was requested to respect her vow.

Confused and upset, the girl gave herself to the very next man who courted her. When she found herself pregnant, she went to another village and later gave birth to a son.

The unwed mother then took her new baby, put him in a basket and left him on the gate of the pagoda where Thi-Kinh was a monk. In a letter she placed in the basket she accused Thi-Kinh as a being the father of the child.

When the superior, surrounded by all of the monks, was reading the note from the unwed mother, Thi-Kinh bent down and picked up the baby because he was screaming. Her natural gesture confirmed the charge in the eyes of the monks and she was expelled from the religious community.

Thi-Kinh would have committed suicide in her despair, but she felt pity for the deserted child and decided that she must resign herself to her fate. She had to resort to begging, tramping up and down the streets every day with the child and a bowl in her hands, asking for alms.

Finally, she could continue no longer. She staggered to the pagoda to knock for the last time at the religious door. She confessed the secrets of her life to the superior and begged him to forgive her for disguising herself as a man in order to become a monk. She also asked that no one be harmed for what they had done to her. She thrust the child, who had become like her own, into the superior's hands for safekeeping and drew her last breath.

The king was told of what had happened. He was so deeply

impressed by the chastity and drive of the unfortunate women that he issued an order to title her "Quan-Am-Tong-Tu," the compassionate protectress of children, and raised her to divinity rank.

(Adapted from a "retelling" by Le-Huy-Hap)

The Lady of Nam-Xuong As a nation that has seldom known relief from war, Vietnam's women have grown accustomed to being left alone and not knowing whether or not they will ever see their husbands alive again. The following legend tells the story of a family in such a situation.

Once upon a time, in the region of Nam-Xuong, there lived a woman whose husband had been sent with the army to a border guard post on the northern front. Communications were almost impossible and she rarely heard from him. She resigned herself to her fate and stayed at home doing agricultural and house-work and looked after their small son. Each evening, she would cast her eyes on the horizon and yearn for her husband to come home.

One winter evening a storm came up creating a frightful noise. Their little house shook with the wind and the oil light blew out, leaving the mother and child in darkness. The child began to scream in fear.

The mother held the child to her breast and re-lit the oil lamp. As she did so, her shadow appeared on the wall and a thought occurred to her. She said to her son, "Don't be afraid, darling, daddy will protect you." She then pointed her finger at the shadow on the wall and said, "see daddy." The little boy looked up at the quivering shadow and stopped crying immediately. His mother hummed a sweet tune and he fell asleep.

The next evening before going to bed, the little boy called for his father. His mother's face lit up with a smile and she placed herself so that her son could see the shadow on the wall again. Then she taught him to clasp his hands in a mark of respect and bow to the shadow and say, "Goodnight, daddy!" This grew into a habit and took place every evening.

Some time later, the man returned to his home and family. His wife was overcome with happiness, but as was traditional with Vietnamese women of her time, she said nothing to reveal her feelings. She could not keep her joy to herself and tears flowed down her cheeks. She said to him, "We must have a thanksgiving to our ancestors, I am going to get some food. Prepare the altar and look after your son and I will be back shortly."

The man began to get acquainted with his little boy. Each time he told the child, "Come, I am your father," the child would refuse and say, "You are not my daddy. Daddy isn't here now and I always say goodnight to my father before I go to bed."

The father was shocked, but was too proud to say anything to his wife. He did nothing and kept quiet. When his wife returned from the market, she had a feeling something was wrong and that misfortune was coming to her home. It had come, indeed! When she spoke to her husband, he turned away in silence. Her usual reserved manner only inflamed the doubt in her husband's heart.

Silently, he prostrated himself before the family ancestral altar and just as silently, he folded up the mat to keep his wife from performing her rites. When the meal was served, he did not even touch the chopsticks or taste a morsel of the food. After the food had cooled, he walked from the house.

His wife spent many days in solitude awaiting his return. One day, she could stand the sorrow no longer and she embraced her child and entrusted him to a neighbor. Then running like a mad woman, she threw herself into the river and drowned.

The death of his wife was a severe shock to the man's cold heart. Suspicion gave away to sorrow. He returned home and claimed his child. One evening when he lit the oil lamp, his own shadow appeared on the wall. To his surprise, he saw his son clasp his little hands together, bow to the shadow and say, "Good-night daddy!"

At once he knew what had happened, but now it was too late to do anything for his poor wife. He had an altar set up on the river bank and three-day and night requiem mass was celebrated.

The man never married again, but spent his entire life caring for and educating his son.

APPENDIX 1: National Slogans

The National Anthem of the Republic of Vietnam

Nậy anh em ổi, Quốc-Gia đến ngãy giãni phóng.
Youth of Vietnam, this is the time we must liberate our country.

Đồng lòng cũng đi, hy sinh tiếc gì thân sống.
Let's all march forward and if need be, repay our nation with our life.

Vì tưởng lai Quốc-Gia, cùng xong pha khói tên
For the future of our country, let us run onto the smokes of battles

lãm sao cho nưởc Nam tử nay luôn vửng bền.
so that our beloved Vietnam will forever remain free and secure.

Dù cho phổi thây trên gưởm giáo
Even if we should perish on the battlefield,

thù nưởc lấý mán đaò đem báo.
we should shed our blood to defend the honor of our country.

Nòi giống lúc biến phãi cân giãi nguy
In the time of crisis we must defend our nation

đoàn thanh niên ta vửng lòng tâm trí
and we, the youth of the nation, must remain firm and determined

hùng tráng quyết chiến đấu làm cho khắp nổi
to fight for our country so that everywhere

van tiếng ngưởi nưởc Nam cho đến muôn đởi.
the good name of Vietnam will live forever.

Anh em ởi, mau hiến thân dưởi cờ.
My friends, let us close ranks under the banner.

Anh em ởi, mau làm cho cõi bờ thóat cởn tàn phá
My friends, let us rid our fatherland of all the destructive forces

vẽ vang đởi sống xứng danh ngàn năm, giống giống Lac Hồng.
and live up to the glorious heritage of our Lac Hong origin.

Coat of Arms of the Republic of Vietnam (South Vietnam)

The coat of arms of the Republic of Vietnam is a clump of bamboo flanked by a paintbrush, symbol of spiritual worth, and a sword, denoting the fighting potential of the Vietnamese people.

The central theme of the emblem is the flexible bamboo, symbolizing consistency, faithfulness, and vitality. Bamboo is abundant in Vietnam and therefore closely associated with the life of her people. It provides a familiar image of home and the way of Vietnamese life.

In addition to spiritual worth, the paintbrush is the general symbol of culture. Likewise, in addition to fighting potential, the sword represents strength and determination.

National Colors of the Republic of Vietnam (South Vietnam)

The National Colors of the Republic of Vietnam consist of three horizontal red stripes on a saffron field. The red color of the stripes are the traditional symbol of Sino-Vietnamese happiness, and represent the three regions of the Republic. The saffron field, as precious as gold, is symbolic of Vietnamese ancestral earth.

APPENDIX 2: Tribal Minorities of Vietnam

South Vietnam's Main Tribes

NAME OF TRIBE	ESTIMATED POPULATION	MISCELLANEOUS INFORMATION
Behnar	90,000	Influential tribe. Their language is used as a trade language for several northern tribes. Has a family system similar to the Western world. People are diversified; from educated office workers to primitive types.
Bru	50,000	Some of the tribe is located in Laos and North Vietnam. Many of its people are sick with malaria and live in tiger infested areas. Christian missionaries have been with this tribe since 1931.
Budip Bulach	7,000 (combined)	Their language is similar to the Mnong tribe. No missionary work being done. They are called "feather people."
Cham	20,000	The Champa empire was vast almost 1,000 years ago in

NAME OF TRIBE	ESTIMATED POPULATION	MISCELLANEOUS INFORMATION
		Vietnam. Some towers from their past still stand in the country. The Chams were defeated by the Vietnamese. Their language is similar to the Chru, Hroi, and southern Raglai tribes. Few are Christians. They are not montagnards.
Chrao	15,000	Little is known about this tribe. Missionaries and Bible translators are working with them.
Chru	18,000	Missionaries have made some progress. There are now over 600 Christians in this tribe.
Cua (Kua)	15,000	Located in the cinnamon producing region.
Gar	8,000	There has been little influence from the outside world on this tribe. Missionary work in this area has been abandoned because of the insurgency. No roads are in the area. The language is very difficult.

NAME OF TRIBE	ESTIMATED POPULATION	MISCELLANEOUS INFORMATION
Halang	30,000	Part of this tribe is located in Laos and Cambodia. No missionary work has been done with this tribe largely due to the lack of roads.
Hroi	10,000	This tribe often call themselves Chams. They live in stilt houses and wear loincloths like the Jarai tribe. Missionary work has been stopped because of the insurgency.
Hrey	120,000	Live in the mountains and the valleys. This is one of the few tribes cultivating rice. A christian mission was established with this tribe in 1958.
Jarai	200,000	This is a very interesting and powerful mountain tribe. Missionaries have worked with this tribe since 1948. (See the main text, Chapter 3 for a more complete discussion of this tribe.)
Jeh	15,000	The area in which this tribe lives is difficult to reach because of the mountains. Some

NAME OF TRIBE	ESTIMATED POPULATION	MISCELLANEOUS INFORMATION
		resettling has occurred allowing more contact with the Western world.
Katu	30,000	This isolated tribe is said to be very primitive, still making human sacrifices. Those on the coastal plains are more civilized and there are several all-Christian villages.
Koho	100,000	This was one of the first tribes to be contacted by Western missionaries. It boasts over 8,000 Christians. The educational and cultural development of this tribe is diversified with the range going from white collar workers to the most primitive of individuals.
Kayong	4,000	This is a small tribe which has little contact with Westerners. Little is known about the tribe.
Mnong	20,000	Part of the tribe is located in Cambodia. The remainder is sparsely scattered over a very large area in South Vietnam.

NAME OF TRIBE	ESTIMATED POPULATION	MISCELLANEOUS INFORMATION
Muong	8,000	This tribe is made up of refugees living near Banmethout and Pleiku. Their tribe in North Vietnam numbers over 210,000. They are closer to the Vietnamese culture than any other tribe; most speak Vietnamese.
Monom	4,000	Little is known about this tribe except that they live along streams in the high mountains of Central Vietnam.
Nung	1,000	This tribe is made up of refugees from North Vietnam; living near Song-Mao. Most speak Vietnamese. The tribe was the subject of a political controversy in 1955.
Pakoh	10,000	A group that is different in that they pluck their eyebrows and tattoo their body.
Raday (Rhade)	120,000	This is considered to be the most influential tribe in the Highland region. It has an interesting marital custom in that the husband goes to live

NAME OF TRIBE	ESTIMATED POPULATION	MISCELLANEOUS INFORMATION
		in the wife's house and takes her name. The wife owns all goods, and the children inherit the mothers estate with preference going to the daughters. It was with this tribe that Christian and Missionary Alliance personnel, including a woman doctor were kidnapped from the leprosarium by the Viet-Cong.
Raglai (Roglai)	40,000	Their language is Layayo-Polynesian with a northern and southern dialect. Many speak Vietnamese.
Sedang	40,000	They live near the highest mountain peak in South Vietnam. Roman Catholic and Protestant missionaries are very active here. The Sedangs live in independent villages.
Stieng	23,000	Many members of this tribe live in Cambodia. They are noted as individualistic and independent minded.

NAME OF TRIBE	ESTIMATED POPULATION	MISCELLANEOUS INFORMATION
Tau-Oi	5,000	Part of the tribe is in Laos. They make more money than most mountain people because of owning elephants.

Some North Vietnamese Tribes

NAME OF TRIBE	ESTIMATED POPULATION	MISCELLANEOUS INFORMATION
Man	2,000,000–4,000,000 (In China and North Vietnam)	This tribe is found in North Vietnam and China. They have a strong family system. Most members of the tribe speak Chinese and some speak Vietnamese. Some have fled to the south and live near Banmethout. The tribe in the north is nomadic.
Muong	211,000	Approximately 8,000 of this tribe have fled south as refugees. Their language is similar to Vietnamese with Quoc Ngu script. They are considered to be much like the Vietnamese in customs and religion.
Nung	Unknown	Over 8,000 came south as refugees. They were involved in political problems when

NAME OF TRIBE	ESTIMATED POPULATION	MISCELLANEOUS INFORMATION
		President Diem was accused of using their troops in crushing sect rebellions in 1955.
Thai	350,000	This tribe lives near the Chinese and Laotian frontiers. They cultivate rice on the plains and in the mountains. Many understand Vietnamese. About 7,000 have fled south as refugees.
Tho	Unknown	They are located along the China border. About 5,000 refugees fled to the south. Many speak Chinese and Vietnamese.

Other tribes in North Vietnam include the Kelao, Laqual, Lati, Lolo, Meo, and Nhang.

APPENDIX 3:
A Physical and Racial Map of Vietnam

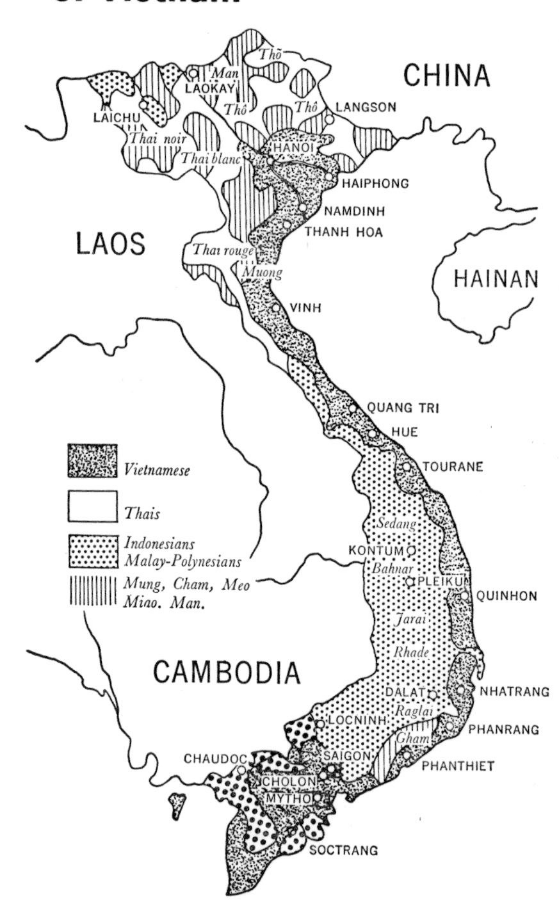

APPENDIX 4: Basic Vietnamese Language

Diacritical Marks

Mark	Inflection	Position
́	Rising inflection	Always above a vowel
̀	Lowering inflection	Always above a vowel
̉	Ever rising inflection	Always above a vowel
̃	Rising and break inflection	Always above a vowel
•	Low inflection	Always below a vowel

EXAMPLE

Ma *Má* *Mà* *Mả* *Mã* *Mạ*

Alphabet

a b c d đ e g h i k l m n o p q r s t u v x y

a ă â e ê o ô u ư ng nh ngh gi gu ph th

Glossary of Selected Vocabulary

One	*Một*	Black	*Đen*
Two	*Hai*	Blue	*Xanh da trời*
Three	*Ba*	Brown	*Nau*
Four	*Bốn*	Green	*Xanh lá cây*
Five	*Năm*	Red	*Đỏ*
Six	*Sáu*	White	*Trắng*
Seven	*Bãy*	Yellow	*Vàng*
Eight	*Tám*	North	*Bắc*
Nine	*Chín*	South	*Nam*
Ten	*Mười*	East	*Đông*
		West	*Tây*

Minute	*Phút*	Miss	*Cô*
Hour	*Giỏ*	Mrs.	*Bà*
Day	*Ngaỳ*	Mr.	*Ông*
Week	*Tuầǹ*	Man	*Ngủỏi đàn ông*
Month	*Tháng*	Woman	*Nguoi dàn bà*
Monday	*Thứ hai*	January	*Tháng giêng*
Tuesday	*Thứ ba*	February	*Tháng haimp*
Wednesday	*Thứ tư*	March	*Tháng ba*
Thursday	*Thứ năm*	April	*Tháng tủ*
Friday	*Thứ sáu*	May	*Tháng năm*
Saturday	*Thứ bẩy*	June	*Tháng sáu*
Sunday	*Chu nhât*	July	*Tháng bãy*
		August	*Tháng tám*
Drink	*Uong*	September	*Tháng chín*
Eat	*Añ*	October	*Tháng mủổi*
Hunger	*Đói*	November	*Tháng mủổi một*
Breakfast	*Ãn sáng, diêm̃ tâm*	December	*Tháng chap*
Lunch	*Cỏm trủa*		

Useful Phrases in Vietnamese

FIRST MEETING

Good morning.	*Chào ông.*
I am Mr. —	*Tôi là—*
Where are we going now?	*Chúng ta đi đâu bây giò?*
Where shall I meet you?	*Tôi sẽ găp ông ỏ đâu?*
How long will you stay?	*Ông sẽ ổ lại bao lâu?*
Good night	*Chào ông.*

QUESTIONS

What is your name?	*Tên ông là gì?*

Where are you from?	*Ông ở dâu dến?*
What are you doing here?	*Ông làm gì ở dấy?*
How old are you?	*Ông bao nhiêu tüoi?*
Where is your family?	*Gia dình của ông ở dau?*
Do you know anyone here?	*Ông có bíêt ai ở dây không?*
Show me some identification.	*Cho tôi xem gíân căn cuốc.*

COMMUNICATION

Hello, This is Mr.—	*Allo, Tôi là—*
Can you hear me?	*Nghe tôi có rõ không?*
Speak louder.	*Nói to hỏn.*
I want to send a message.	*Tôi muốn gủi một thông diệp.*
What is the news?	*Có tin gì không?*

INFORMATION

Show me where we are on the map?	*Chỉ vào bản dồ cho tôi biết hiện nay chúng ta ở dâu.*
Where does this road lead?	*Con dưỏng nây đi đến đâu?*
How far is the next village?	*Còn bao xa nũa đén làng?*
We get food from the village.	*Chúng tôi lấy lủỏng thủc ở trong làng.*
How far is the camp from the city?	*Trai lính ở cách thành phô bao xa?*
How far is it from here to Saigon?	*Tù dây dến Saigon bao xa?*

MEDICAL

Is there a doctor here?	*Ở dây có bác sĩ không?*
Where are you hurt?	*Ông dau ở dâu?*
Don't move.	*Đùng củ dông.*
Take this medicine.	*Dùng thuôc náy.*

Bring the stretcher.	*Đem băng-ca lai dây.*
He needs blood.	*Ông ấy cần máu.*
The wound is infected.	*Vết thủổng có mủ*
Where is the first aid station?	*Tram củú thủổng ổ đâu?*

SECURITY

It is not safe here.	*Ổ dây không dủổc yên.*
Be very quiet.	*Phải im lăng.*
They are surrounded.	*Ho bi bao vây.*
Who are these people with you?	*Nhủng ngủổi kia là ai?*

APPENDIX 5:
Vietnamese Military Ranks and Insignia

Vietnamese Army

INSIGNIA	TITLE	TRANSLATION	U.S. EQUIVALENT
	*Thuong Tuong*	General	General of the Army
	*Dai Tuong*	L/General	General
	*Trung Tuong*	Major General	L/General
	*Thieu Tuong*	Brig/General	Major General
	*Dai Ta*	Colonel	Colonel
	*Trung Ta*	L/Colonel	L/Colonel
	Thieu Ta	Major	Major
	*Dai Uy*	Captain	Captain
	*Trung Uy*	Lieutenant	1st Lieutenant
	Thieu Uy	2nd Lieutenant	2nd Lieutenant
	Chuan Uy	Aspirant	None
	Sinh Vien Quan	Student Officer	Officer Candidate
	Thuong Si I	Chief Warrant Off. M/Sgt. 1st Class	Chief Warrant Off. Sgt. Major, E-9
	Thuong Si	M/Sgt.	First Sergeant
	*Trung Si I*	Sergeant I	Sergeant 1st Class

INSIGNIA	TITLE	TRANSLATION	U.S. EQUIVALENT
	*Trung Si*	Sergeant	Staff Sergeant
	*Ha Si I*	Corporal I	Sergeant
	*Ha Si*	Corporal	Corporal
	*Binh I*	Private I	Private 1st Class
None	*Binh II*	Private	Recruit

Note: Insignia Colors

General Officer—SILVER
Field Grade Officer—SILVER
Company Grade Officer—GOLD
Aspirant and Student Officer—GOLD
Chief Warrant Officer and M/Sgt. 1st Class—GOLD
Sergeant—SILVER
Corporal—SILVER and GOLD
Private—GOLD

Vietnamese Navy and Marine Corps

INSIGNIA	TITLE	TRANSLATION	U.S. EQUIVALENT
	*Do Doc*	Admiral	Admiral
	*Pho Do Doc*	Vice Admiral	Vice Admiral
	*De Doc*	Rear Admiral	Rear Admiral
	*Pho De Doc*	Commodore	Commodore
	*Hai Quan Dai Ta*	Captain	Captain
	*Hai Quan Trung Ta*	Commander	Commander
	*Hai Quan Thieu Ta*	L/Commander	L/Commander
	*Hai Quan Dai Uy*	Lieutenant	Lieutenant
	*Hai Quan Trung Uy*	Lieutenant (J.G.)	Lieutenant (J.G.)

INSIGNIA	TITLE	TRANSLATION	U.S. EQUIVALENT
	*Hai Quan Thieu Uy*	Ensign	Ensign
	*Chuan Uy*	Aspirant	None
	Hai Quan	Midshipman	Midshipman
	Thuong Sy Quan	Chief Warrant Off.	Chief Warrant Off.
	Ha Sy Quan	Warrant Officer	Warrant Officer
	*Thuong Si 1*	High Enlisted 1st Class (P.O.)	Senior Chief Petty Officer
	*Thuong Si*	High Enlisted (P.O.)	Chief Petty Officer
	*Trung Si 1*	Middle Enlisted 1st Class (P.O.)	Petty Officer First Class
	*Trung Si*	Middle Enlisted (P.O.)	Petty Officer Second Class
	Ha Si I (Chuyen Nghiep)	Leading Seaman I (Low enlisted I)	Petty Officer ThirdClass
	Ha Si I	Leading Seaman (Low enlisted I)	Petty Officer Third Class
	Ha Si	Seaman I (Low enlisted)	Seaman
	Thuy Thu I RA *Thuy Thu II RA*	Seaman II (Sailor I & II)	Seaman Apprentice Seaman Apprentice

Note: Insignia Colors
Flag Officers—SILVER
Other Officers—GOLD
Rated Enlisted—GOLD
Seamen—BLUE

Marine Corps—Insignia is metal and identical to Navy, but braid is silver. Ranks of Marine Corps are similar in name to those of the Army

Vietnamese Air Force

INSIGNIA	TITLE	TRANSLATION	U.S. EQUIVALENT
	*Dai Tuong Khong Quan*	L/General	L/General
	*Trung Tuong Khong Quan*	Major General	Major General
	*Thieu Tuong Khong Quan*	Brigadier General	Brigadier General

INSIGNIA	TITLE	TRANSLATION	U.S. EQUIVALENT
	*Dai Ta Khong Quan*	Colonel	Colonel
	*Trung Ta Khong Quan*	L/Colonel	L/Colonel
	Thieu Ta Khong Quan	Major	Major
	*Dai Uy Khong Quan*	Captain	Captain
	*Trung Uy Khong Quan*	1st Lieutenant	1st Lieutenant
	Thieu Uy Khong Quan	2nd Lieutenant	2nd Lieutenant
	Chuan Uy Khong Quan	Aspirant	None
	Sinh Vien Quan	Student Officer	Officer Candidate
	Thuong Sy Quan	Chief Warrant Off.	Chief Warrant Off.
	Ha Sy Quan	Warrant Officer	Warrant Officer
	Thuong Si 1 Khong Quan	Senior Master Sergeant	Senior Master Sergeant
	Thuong Si Khong Quan	Master Sergeant	Master Sergeant
	*Trung Si I Khong Quan*	Technical Sergeant	Technical Sergeant
	*Trung Si Khong Quan*	Staff Sergeant	Staff Sergeant
	*Ha Si I Khong Quan*	Airman First Class	Airman First Class
	*Ha Si Khong Quan*	Airman Second Class	Airman Second Class
	*Binh I Khong Quan*	Airman Third Class	Airman Third Class
None	*Bin II Khong Quan*	Airman Basic	Airman Basic

Note: Insignia Colors

General Officers—SILVER
Field Grade Officers—SILVER
Company Grade Officers—GOLD

Sr. M/Sgt.—GOLD
Sergeants—SILVER
Airman Rated—GOLD

APPENDIX 6: Comparison of Vietnamese and U.S.A. Elementary and Secondary Schooling

Elementary School

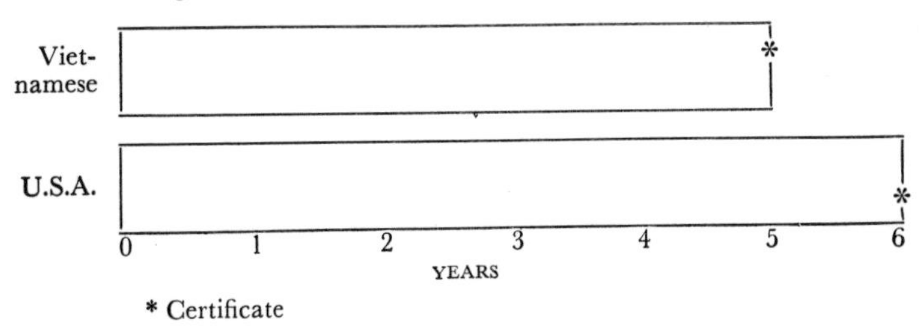

Junior High School

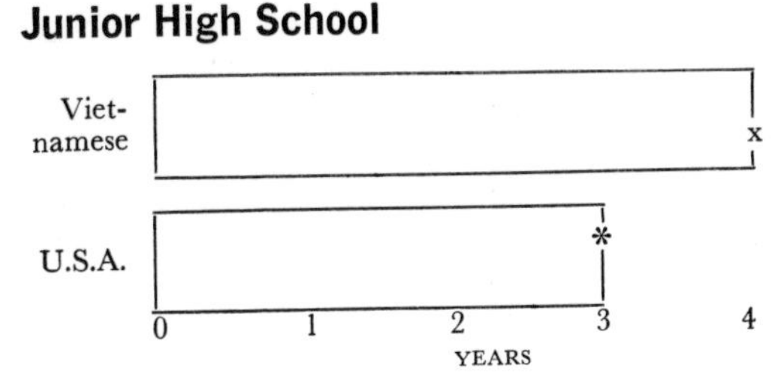

* Diploma

x
(1) Diploma of Indochinese Upper Elem. Studies.
(2) Certificate of Further Elem. Studies.
(3) Certificate of Vocational Skills.
(4) Certificate of Industrial Skills.

Noe: Diploma (1) or Certificate (2) is awarded depending on the academic school chosen and Certificate (3) or (4) depending on the vocational school chosen.

Senior High School

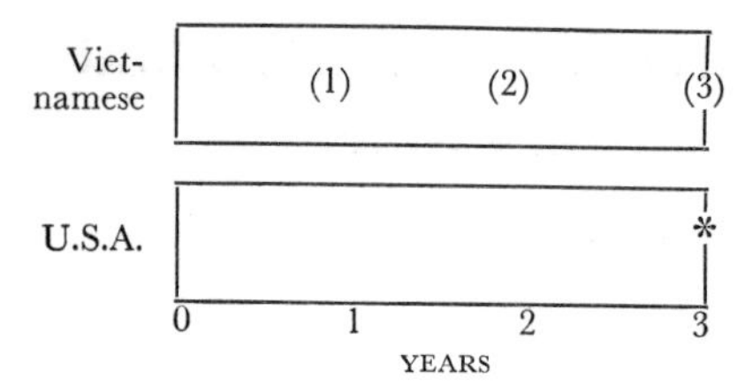

* Diploma
- (1) Diploma Pedagogic Aptitude.
- (2) Diploma Commercial Studies or Baccalaureat, I.
- (3) Baccalaureat, II.

Note: (1) is permitted to teach in the Elementary School.
(2) Diploma of Commercial Studies is awarded by the National School of Commerce.
(3) Required for entrance to all higher education (see Appendix 7).

Post High School

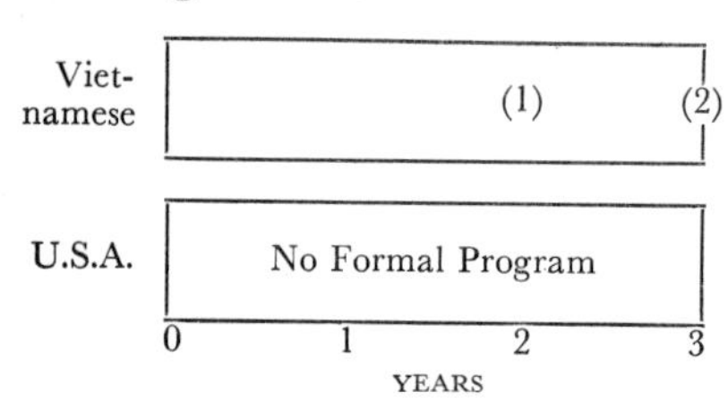

Note: (1) and (2) the title Agent Technique is awarded by the National Technical Center in Civil, Mechanical and Electrical technology at the 2 year and at the 3 year levels.

APPENDIX 7:
Comparison of Vietnamese and U.S.A. Higher Education with Recommended Equivalents Toward U.S.A. Degrees

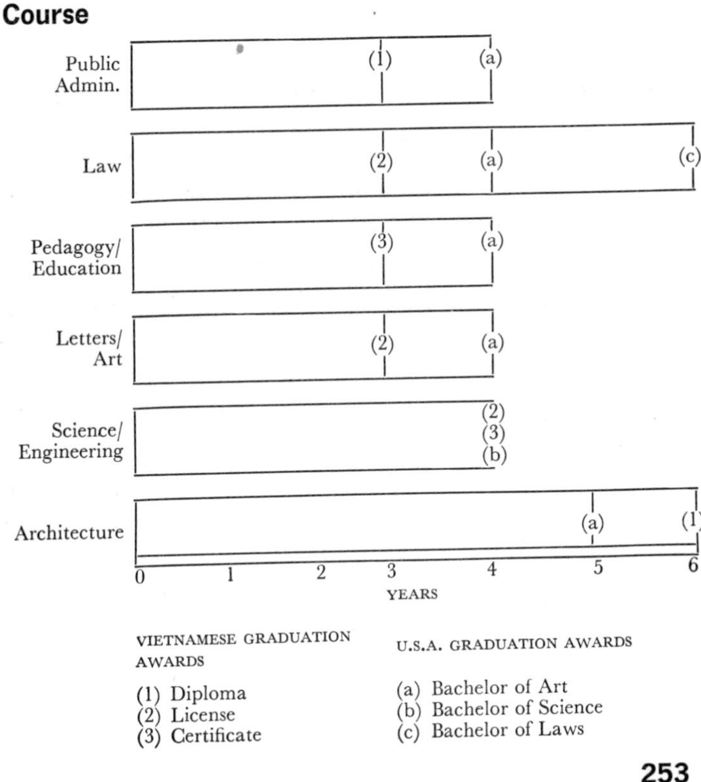

VIETNAMESE GRADUATION AWARDS

(1) Diploma
(2) License
(3) Certificate

U.S.A. GRADUATION AWARDS

(a) Bachelor of Art
(b) Bachelor of Science
(c) Bachelor of Laws

APPENDIX 8: Chronological Table

HISTORICAL PERIOD	NAME AND/OR EVENT
20 millenniums before Christ–2879 B.C.	*Giao Chi:* Peoples from the southern portion of present-day China occupied North Vietnam. The pre-legendary era.
2879–257 B.C.	*Kingdom of Xich-guy:* Emperor Kinh-Duong-Vuong. Empire is bounded by Yang-Tse-Kiang on the north, present-day Vietnam in the south, the west by Seut-Chouan and east by the South China Sea.
257–207 B.C.	*Kingdom of An-Lac:* Emperor Thuc-Duong-Vuong. Capital is at Phong-Khe.
207–111 B.C.	*Kingdom of Nam-Viet (Nam-Yue):* Emperor is Chinese General Trieu-Da. Capital is at Phieu-Ngung. Founded the Trieu Dynasty which reigned during this period.
111 B.C.–A.D. 938	*An-Nam (Do-ho-Phu):* Called the protectorate of the pacified south by the Chinese. *Dai Viet:* The title used by the Vietnamese. The era of the first Chinese domination.

HISTORICAL PERIOD	NAME AND/OR EVENT
(544–602)	*Van-Xuan:* An age of great confusion. The period of the early Vietnamese dynasty of Ly's yet the Chinese hold on in the face of these rivals. To the outside world the name remains *An-Nam.*
938–1054	*Kingdom of Viet:* The early and middle Great National Dynasties beginning with Ngo-Quyen as emperor and ending with Dinh-Bo-Linh.
1054–1164	*Dai-Viet:* This is the title that was used by the Vietnamese during the era of the first Chinese domination.
1164–1802	*An-Nam:* This is the same name used by the first Chinese conquerors. The name is established by the Vietnamese General Tran-Hung-Dao who is a national hero for his fight against the Mongols.
(1400–1428)	*Dai-Ngu:* A title given to the country by Emperor Ho-Quy-Lo who moved his capital to Tay-Do.
(1428–1433)	*Dai Viet:* The same name that was used during the first Chinese domination is bestowed on the country by Le-Thai-To who sets up his capital at Dong-Kinh (Hanoi).

HISTORICAL PERIOD	NAME AND/OR EVENT
1802–1820	*Vietnam:* The first time that the present-day name for the country was used. It was officially adopted in 1804 by the Emperor Gia Long.
1820–1945	*Dai-Nam:* The name used during the pre-French and French domination eras.
1945–1948	*Democratic Republic of Vietnam:* This name was given official status by the abdication at Hue, on August 25, 1945, of His Majesty Bao-Dai to Viet-Minh representatives.
1948–1954	*State of Vietnam:* Bao-Dai is made Chief of State within the French Union.
1954–present	*The Republic of Vietnam:* The Geneva Agreement signed on July 21, 1954 ended hostilities in Indochina and partitioned the country at approximately the 17th parallel into the free *Republic of Vietnam* in the south and the communist *Democratic Republic of Vietnam* in the north.

BIBLIOGRAPHY

Public Documents

International Voluntary Services, Vietnam. *Annual Report, June 1962–June 1963,* Saigon, Undated.

Republic of Vietnam, Department of National Economy, Industrial Development Center. *Investing in Vietnam,* Saigon, Undated.

Republic of Vietnam, Department of National Education. *Review Horizons,* Vietnam Culture Series, Varied, Saigon, Undated.

United States of America, United States Operations Mission, Vietnam. *An Interim Report of the Cholera Epidemic, December 20, 1963–April 30, 1964,* Saigon, July 1, 1964.

United States of America, United States Operations Mission, Vietnam. *Annual Statistical Bulletin, No. 7,* (Data through 1963), Saigon, July 1964.

United States of America, United States Operations Mission, Vietnam. *Health Contributes to the Progress of a Nation,* (Annual Report of the Public Health Division), July 1, 1962.

United States of America, United States Operations Mission, Vietnam. *Student Records from Vietnam,* Saigon, April 1962.

United States of America, United States Operations Mission, Vietnam. *Studies in Vietnamese Economy, Vol. I,* Ed. Alek A. Rozental, Saigon, 1964.

United States of America, United States Operations Mission, Vietnam. *The U. S. Assistance Program for Vietnam,* Saigon, January 1965.

Periodicals Containing Articles on Vietnam

Asian Student. Weekly, San Francisco.

Bangkok World. Daily, Bangkok.

China Quarterly. Congress for Cultural Freedom, London.

Far Eastern Economic Review. Weekly, Hong Kong.

Free World. Monthly, Free Asia Press, Manila.

Huong Que. Monthly, 145 Dai-Lo Nguyen-Hue, Saigon.

Jungle Frontiers. Seasonal, Christian and Missionary Alliance, New York.

Philippines Herald. Daily, Manila.

Philippines Herald Magazine. Weekly, Manila.

Saigon Daily News. Daily, Saigon.

Saigon Post. Daily, Saigon.

Saigon Round-Up. Weekly, Saigon.

The Call. Bi-annually, Vietnam Missionaries of the Christian and Missionary Alliance, New York.

Books

Buttinger, Joseph. *The Smaller Dragon: A Political History of Vietnam,* Praeger: New York, 1958.

Dooley, T. A. *Deliver Us From Evil: The Story of Vietnamese Flight to Freedom,* Farrar, Straus and Cudahy: New York, 1956.

Fall, Bernard B. *The Two Viet Nams: A Political and Military Analysis,* Praeger: New York, 1963.

Fisher, C. A. *South-East Asia: A Social, Economic and Political Geography,* Methuen: London, 1964.

Fitch, Florence Mary. *Their Search for God: Ways of Worship in the Orient,* Lothrop: New York, 1947.

Groslier, B. P. *The Art of Indochina,* Crown: New York, 1962.

Hammer, E. J. *The Struggle for Indochina,* Stanford University Press: Stanford, 1954.

Hickey, Gerald G. *The Study of a Vietnamese Rural Community-Sociology,* Michigan State University: Saigon, 1960.

Hoa, Nguyen-Dinh. *Read Vietnamese: A Graded Course in Written Vietnamese,* Tuttle: Rutland, Vermont and Tokyo, 1966.

Hoa, Nguyen-Dinh. *Easy Vietnamese,* Tuttle: Rutland, Vermont and Tokyo, 1966.

Hoa, Nguyen-Dinh. *Speak Vietnamese (revised edition),* Tuttle: Rutland, Vermont and Tokyo, 1966.

Hoa, Nguyen-Dinh. *Vietnamese-English Dictionary,* Tuttle: Rutland, Vermont and Tokyo, 1966.

Lan-Bach, L. T. *Vietnamese Legends,* Kim-Lai-An-Quan: Saigon, 1958.

Minh, Do Van. *Viet Nam Where East and West Meet,* Amilcare Pizzi: Milano, undated.

Schultz, George F. *Vietnamese Legends,* Tuttle: Rutland, Vermont and Tokyo, 1965.

Sivaram, M. *The Vietnam War: Why?* Tuttle: Rutland, Vermont and Tokyo, 1966.

Thai Van Kiem. *Viet Nam Past and Present,* Commercial Transworld Editions: Tangiers, 1952.

Tran, Van Tung. *Viet Nam,* Praeger: New York, 1959.

White, John. *History of a Voyage to the China Sea,* Wells and Lilly: Boston, 1820.

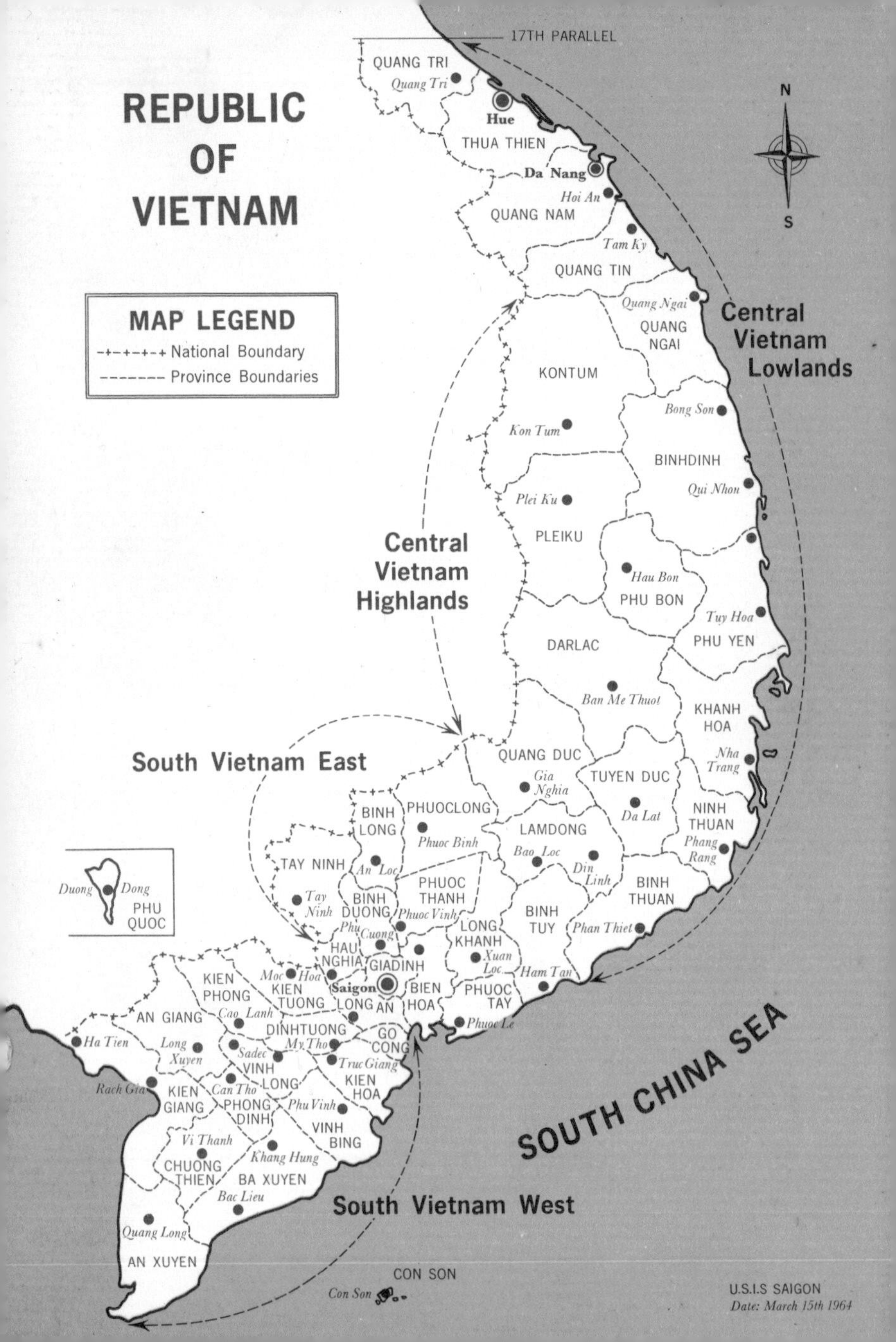

REPUBLIC OF VIETNAM
MAP LEGEND
National Boundary
Province Boundaries
17TH PARALLEL
N
S
QUANG TRI
Quang Tri
Hue
THUA THIEN
Da Nang
Hoi An
QUANG NAM
Tam Ky
QUANG TIN
Quang Ngai
QUANG NGAI
Central Vietnam Lowlands
KONTUM
Kon Tum
Bong Son
BINHDINH
Qui Nhon
Plei Ku
PLEIKU
Central Vietnam Highlands
Hau Bon
PHU BON
Tuy Hoa
PHU YEN
DARLAC
Ban Me Thuot
KHANH HOA
Nha Trang
QUANG DUC
Gia Nghia
TUYEN DUC
Da Lat
NINH THUAN
Phang Rang
South Vietnam East
BINH LONG
PHUOCLONG
Phuoc Binh
LAMDONG
Bao Loc
Din Linh
TAY NINH
An Loc
PHUOC THANH
BINH DUONG
Phuoc Vinh
Tay Ninh
BINH TUY
BINH THUAN
Phan Thiet
Duong Dong
PHU QUOC
Phu Cuong
HAU NGHIA
LONG KHANH
Xuan Loc
GIADINH
Ham Tan
KIEN PHONG
Moc Hoa
KIEN TUONG
Saigon
BIEN HOA
PHUOC TAY
LONG AN
AN GIANG
Cao Lanh
DINHTUONG
Phuoc Le
Ha Tien
Long Xuyen
Sadec
My Tho
GO CONG
VINH LONG
Truc Giang
Rach Gia
KIEN GIANG
Can Tho
PHONG DINH
KIEN HOA
Phu Vinh
VINH BING
Vi Thanh
Khang Hung
CHUONG THIEN
BA XUYEN
Bac Lieu
SOUTH CHINA SEA
South Vietnam West
Quang Long
AN XUYEN
CON SON
Con Son
U.S.I.S SAIGON
Date: March 15th 1964